Nicky Fifth Says

Vote For
T-Bone

by Lisa Funari-Willever

Franklin Mason Press
Columbus, New Jersey

*To New Jersey's children, the future of our amazing state,
understand before speaking, listen patiently, respect others, and
participate in this gift of a democratic government.*

*Special thanks to Anne Salvatore, Wanda Swanson, Dawn Hiltner,
Jennifer Wahner, Iris Hutchinson and Allyssa Barnes,
...amazing women.*

Franklin Mason Press ISBN 978-0-9857218-0-0
Library of Congress Control Number: 2012915684

Printed and Published in the
United States of America

Text copyright © 2012 by Lisa Funari Willever
Cover Artwork by Lauren Lambiase
Cover Design by Peri Gabriel www.knockoutbooks.com

Editorial and Production Staff: Jennifer Wahner, Shoshana   Hurwitz,
Linda Funari, Iris Hutchinson, Kia Santoro, Maribeth Holliday, Darla
Stabler, Allyssa Barnes, Marcia Jacobs, and Mary Sullivan.

No part of this publication may be reproduced, or stored in a retrieval
system, or transmitted in any form or by any means, electronic,
mechanical, photocopying, recording, or otherwise, without written
permission of the publisher. For information regarding permission,
write to FMP, Permissions, 415 Route 68, Columbus, NJ 08022.

www.franklinmasonpress.com
www.nickyfifth.com

Table of Contents

The Nicky Fifth Series

NICKY FIFTH'S
PASSPORT

N**P**F

Visit nickyfifth.com.

Download and print your free Nicky Fifth Passport. Use it when you visit the real NJ locations that the Nicky Fifth characters visit.

Chapter One

The New Jersey Hall of Fame

"Nick! Nick, Nick, are you home?" a voice hollered from the bottom of the stairs, followed by fifteen pounding steps that grew increasingly louder. Soon the steps led the voice to my bedroom door. "Nick, are you here?"

"Really, T-Bone?" I asked. "You do know we have a doorbell, right?"

"I practically live here," he said, shaking his head. "Of course, I know we have a doorbell. I just didn't think anyone was home."

"Did my mom let you in?"

"No, but she left you a note at the bottom of the stairs."

"Where is it?" I asked.

"Out the door, make a left in the hall, and then go down," he answered.

"I know where the bottom of the stairs are," I said, running past him and grabbing the note.

"Your mom ran to the store and said that you were, and I quote, sleeping like a baby and she didn't have the heart to wake you up. Anyway, she'll be right back."

"Very funny," I said as I read the note. "So, if my mom ran out, and clearly locked the door, how did you get in?"

"I used the emergency key," T-Bone explained as if everyone uses the emergency-hidden-under-the-bushes-in-the-fakest-looking-rock-in-the-world-key to visit a friend.

"So what's your emergency?" I asked, almost sounding like a dispatcher from the show COPS.

"It's not exactly an emergency," he shrugged, "it's

more of an importancy."

"Not a word," I corrected.

"I'll check on that later, but I made a big decision today."

"You're switching from Velcro to laces?" I guessed.

"No, I did that last year," he smiled, "although I do miss them. They sure were a time-saver. No, I made a decision to be a politician."

"Let me get this straight," I interrupted. "You broke into my house to tell me that one day, when you're an adult, you want to be a politician? You know we have a phone, right?"

"First of all," he began, "it's getting a little insulting that you keep asking me house inventory questions. Yes, I know we have a doorbell and a phone and an emergency key. And, no, I'm not waiting until I'm an adult."

"Okay, so maybe the real question is, why do you keep saying you know what we have? You know you don't live here, right?"

"Of course, I don't actually live here," he agreed.

"This is more of a vacation home."

"Go back," I instructed, "to the part where you said you weren't waiting to become an adult."

He ran out to the hallway and dragged in a bunch of posters. They were red, white, and blue and they were homemade. One said Vote For T-Bone, another said T-Bone Time, and the last said I Approve This Message.

I was speechless. I literally could not think of one word to say. The awkward pause extended into an awkward silence and through it all, he stood there smiling at me. Clearly, I was supposed to jump up and down or high five him or at the very least, blink. But I had nothing; I was totally, inexcusably speechless.

"Are you shocked? Are you surprised? Do you have so many things running through your head that you don't know which to say first?"

Yeah, that was it, I laughed to myself. Only T-Bone could believe that the reason I was staring blankly was because I had too many thoughts. He should have known me by now. After my family moved from Philadelphia to Dandelion Court, I was devastated. It was T-Bone that made my new life in New Jersey better. We met on the school bus, lived in the same neighborhood, went to the same school, started an odd-job business together, and were even about to be named Official Junior Ambassadors of the state. That was definitely enough time to get to know someone. Too many thoughts, I wondered. That was hardly the reason. On the other hand, it would certainly get me out of an immediate jam, so I happily went with it.

"Totally too many thoughts," I agreed, unable to take my eyes off of his smile. "Hey, are your teeth whiter?"

"Funny you should mention that," he nodded. "I secretly switched my toothpaste a few months ago and I believe I'm at least three shades whiter."

"What do you mean you secretly switched your toothpaste? You can't secretly switch something on yourself," I pointed out.

"Why not?" he asked.

"Because it can't be a secret if you know about it and you're doing it to yourself," I said.

"I knew about the switch," he laughed, "but my teeth didn't. They had no idea."

"Wow," I shook my head. "Onto my next question, why is your head browner than your arms?"

"I started using my mom's bronzing lotion," he said matter-of-factly. "The bottle said it will give me a healthy glow and my brother said it will make my teeth look whiter."

"Yeah, but you're head doesn't match your neck," I observed. I moved in for a closer look, more speechless now than I was before.

"That's what I wanted to talk to you about," he continued.

"You wanted to talk to me about how your head and neck are different colors and your teeth look like you plugged them in?"

"No, I want you to be my campaign manager."

"Huh?" I said as I finally blinked.

"Nick, I'm a big picture guy. I have big, bold ideas and I need a detail guy. I need someone who can take one look at me and see my head and neck don't match. Nick, I need someone I trust to run this campaign and help me get elected and you're that someone."

"Huh?" I repeated.

"Nick, I'm not gonna lie to you. It's gonna be hard work and long hours, but I think we can do it. Whaddya say? Are you in?"

"What are you talking about? Am I in what?" I asked.

"Will you be my campaign manager?" he replied as if his was the most normal request in the world.

"A. I don't know anything about being a campaign manager. B. How can you run for office when you have to be 18 years old to vote? And C. Have you lost your mind?"

"Well, that will be our first order of business. You can help me find the right election. And don't worry about what you know, I mean, how hard can it be?"

"You seriously made posters and wanna start a campaign and you don't even know what you want to run for?"

"Exactly," he nodded.

"Then yes, of course I'll run your campaign," I said

in my most sarcastic voice. "How do you feel about president?"

"Nick, I think you're shooting a little high there. You need to be more realistic."

"You're really going to stand there and tell me that I need to be more realistic?" I laughed. "Okay, my apologies. I guess we shouldn't start at the top. How about Governor?"

"Still shooting high," he replied after giving it some thought. "I'm thinking state senator or assembly-man, you know, to get my feet wet."

"Follow me," I said as I ran to the family room and logged onto the computer. I searched the minimum age to run for Senator or Assemblyman in New Jersey. "Here it is and it's good news."

"I'm old enough to run?" he asked.

"No, you must be 21 years old to run for the General Assembly and 30 years old to run for the Senate."

"How is that good?" he asked, suddenly looking dejected.

"We'll have plenty of time to get your campaign ready," I laughed. T-Bone wasn't laughing. He dropped his posters and sank down in my chair. It suddenly hit me that he was completely serious when he broke in my house to announce his candidacy for nothing and to ask me to be his campaign manager. I had seen this look before. It didn't matter how crazy I thought he was, he wouldn't cheer up until I agreed to manage his campaign. But first we had to find an election he was eligible to run in.

We spent an hour searching all of the minimum age requirements for everything from mayor to town council and from district attorney to judge. We learned that to run for a public office you need to live in that district and the age range started at 18 years old and then went up from there. For some positions you needed certain qualifications. For instance, to be a judge, you needed a law degree. That seemed fair. What didn't seem fair was that kids our age really didn't have a voice. I figured most adults assume kids would vote for things like longer summers or ice cream for dinner, which actually weren't bad ideas, but T-Bone did want to know about real issues.

"It's useless," he shrugged. "Unless, hold on, what about the New Jersey Hall of Fame? Every year the public votes on people from New Jersey that have done outstanding things. What if I start doing outstanding things and people nominate me?"

"T-Bone," I started, trying not to hurt his feelings, "it's called the Hall of Fame because it showcases *famous* people from New Jersey."

"Go to their website and let's just see how famous the nominees really are," he instructed, starting to perk up.

"It's www.njhalloffame.org."

"How do you know that?"

"I visit their website a lot," he explained. "Check out the last list of nominees. Do you know all of their names?"

"No," I admitted, "not all of them. But I'm sure some of them are from before our time."

"No, trust me," he insisted. "These people did amazing things, but they all weren't famous. Sure some are athletes and musicians, some are even movie stars, but some are important writers, scientists, and business people."

"I hate to point out the obvious," I began, "but you are, let's just say, none of the above."

"Details, my friend, details."

Oh no, I thought. That's the same phrase he tossed around when we collected stickers for my parents' anniversary gift. It was even the same fake Jamaican accent.

"You're still fakin' Jamaican?" I laughed. "And what are these details you're talking about?"

"The Hall of Fame doesn't require you to be anything in particular and I don't see a minimum age. Look at this," he began reading, "any citizen of the State of New Jersey may nominate an individual, living or deceased, to be considered for induction into the New Jersey Hall of Fame. Teams or musical ensembles will be considered for nomination starting with the Class of 2012."

"There must be some requirements besides being dead or alive," I insisted.

"Look," he continued. "Here are the eligibility requirements. Nominees must have been born in New Jersey or have resided in New Jersey for at least five years and have a strong association with the state. It must be demonstrated that nominees have made a significant contribution to New Jersey, the country or the world."

"Move over," I said, "grabbing the mouse and scrolling down the page. I was desperately trying to find any reason he could not be nominated before he got way too excited. "Okay, let's look at some of the inductees. Marconi invented the wireless radio, Walt Whitman was a poet and they named a bridge near my old house after him, and Jon Bon Jovi, is an amazing musician and a very generous philanthropist."

"Jon Bon Jovi is also an eye doctor?" gasped T-Bone. "Talk about well-rounded."

"No, he's not an optometrist, he's a philanthropist. That means he donates money to good causes."

"I have a sock for donating money, too" he offered.

"I think Bon Jovi gives away a little more than what's in your sock," I shrugged.

"There's Shaquille O'Neal, basketball player and actor, Bud Abbott and Lou Costello, actors and comedians, F. Scott Fitzgerald, a famous author, and Carl Sagan, a scientist that worked with

NASA. And those are just some from the Inaugural Class in 2008."

"I know. They're really amazing, aren't they?"

"Yeah, they're all amazing. So do you see the problem?" I asked, assuming by now that he would realize he was a little out of his league and give up.

"Of course," he said. "The problem is that I didn't know what category I belong in. What do you think?"

I wanted to ask if they had a crazy category, but I didn't want him to start sulking again. I decided to point out the section of the website that explains the five categories. "The Voting Academy votes on a list of nominees compiled by a panel of experts in five categories: Sports, Arts & Entertainment, Historical, General and Enterprise."

T-Bone was unfazed and started methodically eliminating the categories he felt weren't a good fit for his many achievements. "Let's see, Sports would probably be a no and Arts & Entertainment would probably also be a no. When I made my mom a macaroni necklace in first grade I glued it to my hand and my shirt."

"That was arts and crafts," I corrected.

"I'm a history buff and as Junior Ambassadors we've been getting kids excited about history," he mumbled out loud.

"What do you think about history?"

"I think you'd have to actually be historical," I said.

"Good point," he continued. "I guess that leaves me with General and Enterprise. Since they both sound good, should we flip a coin?"

"Do you even know what Enterprise is?" I asked. "It says here that it's open to scientists, business leaders, entrepreneurs, inventors, leaders in medicine, and philanthropists. And no, our odd job business would definitely not qualify you as a business leader."

"Then general it is," he said as he grabbed his posters and a sharpie. He placed the Vote for T-Bone poster on top of the pile and started writing. When he finished, he turned the poster around and blinded me with his extra bright pearly whites. He had inserted one word: *General*. Unfortunately, he inserted it above his name.

Vote For
General
T-Bone

Later that evening, my dad asked me what was going on with T-Bone. I told him that he wanted to run for office, but realized the only office he could possibly be elected to was the New Jersey Hall of Fame. My parents both stopped and looked at each other.

"No, why did he look like a fudgesicle?" my dad squinted.

"What are you talking about?" asked my mother. "Tommy was gone before I came home. Why would you say he looked like a popsicle?"

"Fudgesicle," corrected my dad. "It was most definitely a fudgesicle. He had a dark brown head and his neck looked like a wooden popsicle stick."

I hadn't thought about it like that, but my dad raised a good point. He did look like a fudgesicle.

 "He used his mom's bronzing lotion before he came over so the whole time he was here, he kept getting darker and darker and darker," I explained.

"Why'd he use his mom's bronzing lotion?" asked my dad.

"He wanted his teeth whiter and thought the whitening toothpaste only made him three shades brighter."

"Why is he so worried about having his teeth brighter?" wondered my mom.

"He says he needs really white teeth to be a politician and his brother told him that being very tan can help give the illusion of whiter teeth."

"I'm lost," my dad shook his head. "T-Bone wants to run for office, realized he's too young, and now wants to run for the NJ Hall of Fame?"

"And," my mom interrupted, "he thinks to be elected to any office he needs super white teeth, so he's self-tanning to make his skin darker which will make his teeth whiter?"

"Yes and yes," I answered. "That doesn't make regular sense, but it does make T-Bone sense."

"Nick, I've followed the NJ Hall of Fame since the first Class in 2008. People are nominated and then the public votes on who will be inducted. They're not being elected to an office," my dad explained.

"So there's absolutely nothing he can run for?" I asked, knowing how sad he would be when I told him the news.

"Honey, haven't you overlooked the obvious?" my mom smiled. "Tommy should run for student council."

"No way," said my dad. "Tommy? Tommy, in Student Council? If he really wants to run for something, tell him to run for track."

I couldn't believe we hadn't thought of that. My mom was right, it was so obvious. I ran from the kitchen and back to my room. I grabbed a sharpie, crossed out the word *General*, and replaced it with *President*. I knew when he saw it he would think I had lost my mind. Now, he'd know how I always feel. I called him to tell him my great idea.

"So do I," he said. "I think we should raise money for the New Jersey Hall of Fame's Mobile Museum. So many schools can't afford field trips and buses. Their Mobile Museum not only teaches about New Jersey, but it comes to the schools. Now that's a bargain."

"What are you talking about?" I asked, assuming we were talking about running for office.

"I have to step up my game if I want to be elected to the Hall of Fame," he explained. "I'll need to be twice the ambassador I was before and show them that I'm worthy."

"No, that's why I called you. I talked to my parents and my mom had a great idea. We think you should run for student council," I suggested.

"But I'm kind of getting used to the idea of being a Jersey Hall of Famer. Did you know the actor Michael Douglas was in 2012's class? And Judy Blume was in the Class of 2010. It's an amazing list of New Jersey astronauts, actors, musicians, athletes, writers, artists, scientists, and business leaders. I'd like to be in their club."

"Sure, who wouldn't?" I began. "But you have to do something extraordinary to get nominated and then people have to know about you and vote you in."

"No," he protested, "they have a biography next to every nominee. People can just read all about me."

Sometimes there was no reasoning with him and this was one of those times. I decided to make an executive decision. I decided, as his campaign manager, the only way to make sure he actually heard me was to talk in some kind of campaign lingo like I've seen in old movies. I even took out a small white board like I've seen on the news during the election results.

"Listen, T-Bone," I said in a firm, campaign-managerish voice, "you'll need a resume for the Hall of Fame to take you seriously. We're partners in our odd-job business, so that makes you a very young entrepreneur. That's a good thing. We're also Junior Ambassadors of New Jersey. We make a difference and we're getting people excited about our state. That's also good. But you need more."

"Hey, wait a minute," he interrupted. "You're all those things, too. You're not thinking of running, are you?"

"My only goal is to help you get elected," I laughed. "Stop worrying about me and start focusing on the campaign."

"Really?" he asked. "We're making a run for student council? And you'll be my campaign manager?"

"Yes and yes," I answered. "But we have to make

sure it doesn't interfere with school work, being ambassadors, or our business."

"Piece of cake," he answered as he hung up. "Piece of cake."

Chapter Two

The Big Idea

Luckily, I was able to convince T-Bone that people don't actually run for the Hall of Fame. Now, I just had to hope that he could win the student council election. School was starting soon so I went online to print the list of school supplies and find information for student council. I found both, printed them out and started reading. It wasn't too complicated, at all. If T-Bone wanted to run for student council he would simply have to fill out a form. The kid with the highest number of votes becomes the President, the second highest would be the Vice President, and the third and fourth highest would be Secretary and Treasurer. Basically, T-Bone only needed to come out in the top four to be happy. Anyone who came in after fourth place served as at At-Large Representative, representing the whole school. Even if he didn't win first, I assumed he'd be happy with the other positions.

When I finished, I remembered the pile of envelopes Billy had sent over. Billy worked in the Governor's Office and we became friends when the Governor asked us to be New Jersey's Unofficial Junior Ambassadors. In the beginning, we brought him reports and pictures of the amazing places we visited. Now, he sent us fan mail and ideas from people all over the state. I decided to open some of the envelopes. With a few exceptions, they were really good ideas. I was thrilled that people were visiting the places we wrote about and happy to listen to their advice.

I made a pile for each category: thank you letters, good ideas, maybe ideas, not-so-great ideas, and really weird ones. When T-Bone returned, he wondered why I had so many piles. When I explained my theory, he headed straight for the weird ones.

"This one's funny," he laughed. "Some kid wants us to come see his collection of frogs. He said his mom won't let him bring them inside so he keeps them in the woods."

"I'll pass," I said, imagining families marching into the woods behind her house in search of frogs. "At least he lives in Jersey. This kid suggested we go to Orlando."

"That's ironic," T-Bone pointed out. "You spent your first months in New Jersey trying to convince your parents to spring for an Orlando vacation. Actually, since we started our Garden State adventures, I can't remember you saying the word Orlando once."

He was right. When we moved out of Philadelphia, I thought they owed me a great vacation in Orlando. I even had my brother and sisters make posters and sing annoying songs to drive the point home. Instead of a week in Florida, my parents gave us a vacation that consisted of seven, once-a-week New Jersey day trips. I hated the whole idea. It turned out, they were amazing.

"Look at this!" I yelled, holding a large gold envelope. "It's from an entire class."

"Seriously?" he asked, not sure whether to believe me.

"Actually, no it's not from an entire class," I mumbled while skimming the cover letter.

"Wow, you almost had me there," he shook his head. "How awesome would that have been if it was from a whole class?"

"As awesome as a whole grade level?" I smiled.

"Seriously?" he asked again.

"This package is from the Katharine D. Malone School in Rockaway, New Jersey."

"Wait," T-Bone interrupted, "didn't we go there? Isn't that near the Hibernia Diner?"

"Yup," I replied as I kept reading.

"Are they telling us about another diner we should try? Did the Hibernia Diner open up a second location? Please, tell me it's near here."

"No, they wrote a song about us," I said, wrapping my head around the fact that a grade level knew about us.

"Seriously?" he asked for the third time. "What does they letter say?"

"It's from the fourth graders and their teachers. They really want us to be named Official Junior

Ambassadors as soon as possible. They sent us a copy of their song and dance and they already sent copies to the state house."

"Seriously?"

"Okay, stop saying seriously," I sighed. "And it says here that they follow our adventures on the state website. They even get their parents to visit places we write about. The teachers actually drag their own families to the places we visit. They also sent a memory stick; let's go to the family room and we can watch it on the computer."

We ran downstairs to see the song and dance we inspired. It was awesome. They used the melody from London Bridges, but made up their own New Jersey words. The students were spread out over a map of the United States on the school playground. I was shocked. It was the best song and dance I had ever seen. We watched it so much that we couldn't get the song out of our heads.

Nicky and T-Bone are NOT Official!
Are NOT Official
Are NOT Official,
Nicky and T-Bone are NOT Official!
Come on, Lawmakers. Let's get voting!

Junior ambassadors, yes they are!
Yes they are!
Yes they are!
Junior ambassadors, yes they are!
If you'll only take the vote!

The Glass Museum in Whea-ton, Whea-ton, Whea-ton,
The Cities of Trenton and Burlington
These are just some of their stops.

Wild West City and Morristown, Morristown, Morristown,
Grounds for Sculpture and Lambertville,
Don't forget the Hibernia Diner!

Lot's of beaches – love Cape May, love Cape May, love Cape May
Lot's of beaches – love Cape may,
Cast your vote To Day!

Dance: Everybody clap your hands,
do the T-Bone, ya' all.
To the right this time, to the left this time.
Criss-cross, criss-cross.
Vote Yes!

I'm not exactly sure when it happened, but at some point my sisters, Maggie and Emma came over, followed by my brother, Timmy. Before long, we were all singing and doing the T-Bone. Luckily, we weren't looking for jobs as dancers because we were awful. It didn't matter, though. We were singing and dancing to a song that was written about us. Each time the song ended, Emma yelled, "Again!" and we played it again. Soon, my mom came in from the kitchen. She had a towel over her shoulder and a wooden spoon in her hand as she joined the mayhem. We were having such a good time that no one heard my dad come in from work. That was right about the point where I started adding spins to my routine. One spin didn't make it all the way around and I stopped right in front of him. He was speechless and I was embarrassed, at least for a second. Then I remembered that I inspired the song and I jumped back in.

"Honey?" he yelled to my mom. "Honey, can I have a word with you?"

"Sorry, I'm going to the right and then I'm going to the left. I think I finally got this," she said as she tossed him the spoon. "Can you stir the sauce for me?"

My poor dad had no idea what he had walked in on and he looked too scared to find out. After a few more minutes we all stopped and headed into the kitchen.

"What is going on?" he asked.

"Honestly, hon," my mom said as she tried to catch her breath, "I have no idea."

"Mr. A., it's unbelievable," said T-Bone. "An entire fourth grade in Rockaway made up a song and dance to convince New Jersey's lawmakers to vote for us."

"Hopefully not for best singers and dancers," he said as he sorted the mail.

"No, for Official Junior Ambassadors!" T-Bone replied, throwing his fist in the air.

"Yeah," Emma yelled, "for otis shell Jupiter plastic doors."

"Is that what that was?" my mom asked, more impressed than when she was singing and dancing. "Boys, that's quite an honor."

"Do you think they've been dancing at the state house?" T-Bone pictured a dance party in the Senate Chambers.

"They better not be," my dad answered as he headed to the stairs. "For all the money I pay in taxes, they better be working and not signing or dancing. You know, it's not supposed to be *New Jersey Government, the Musical.*"

"What's with ol' grumpalumps?" T-Bone whispered as my dad's mumbling trailed off in the distance.

T-Bone didn't know it, but my dad wasn't a fan of politics. It was the one topic my mom always avoided. I wasn't sure what his gripe was, but I remembered watching the news with him and he would yell at the television. I never knew what he was so mad about, but he used to yell things like bum and crook. It was probably why he suggested T-Bone run for track instead of student council.

When we went back to my room, we were too excited to keep looking at the piles. We decided to call my Pop to tell him about Rockaway fourth graders. We put him on speakerphone so we could both hear him. He wasn't surprised that so many people were paying attention to what we were doing, but he was excited for us.

"That brings up a good question," he began. "Where's the next trip? And Tommy, as much as we love it, you can't pick Carlo's Bakery again."

"Aw, c'mon," he replied. "I'll bet you Buddy already

misses me and my whisk."

"I doubt that," I shrugged.

"Well, Tessy Colegrove enjoys my company," he insisted. "She knows class when she sees it."

"Maybe she needs glasses," I suggested. "Anyway, Pop, we're not sure where the next day trip will be yet. We have a ton of ideas to go through."

"From our fans," T-Bone added. "They're from our fans."

"And T-Bone's running for student council, too," I said.

"Really," my grandfather asked. "You didn't tell your dad yet, did you, Nick?"

"Too late," I said.

"Tommy, no matter what my son says," said Pop, "let it go in one ear and out of the other."

"I don't get it," said T-Bone.

"I already told you, my dad is not a big fan of politicians," I explained. "He thinks they're all bums and crooks."

"Are they?" T-Bone asked with a look of horror, as if being elected meant he would automatically become a bum or a crook.

"Of course not," my grandfather started laughing. "Politicians are no different than anyone else. You have your good ones and your bad ones. And like everything else in life, the bad ones always get more attention. I'm sure you'll be a good one."

"Okay," T-Bone mumbled, even though he still looked shocked.

"Hey, Pop," I said, "do you think we should call Rockaway and thank them?"

"Sounds like the right thing to do," he agreed.

I looked for a phone number next to the teachers' name. There was Pat Jaremack, June Beck, Dawn Frauenpreis, and Mrs. O'Donnel. I called the number listed and a very happy lady answered the phone.

"Hello," she said as if she were singing the word.

"Um, I'm looking for Mrs. Jaremack. My name is,

um, Nicky and my friend, T-Bone, well we wanted to, um," I began with my usual speaking elegance. Luckily, it didn't matter. As soon as she heard our names, she took over.

"Oh my Gosh, is this Nicky and T-Bone?" the voice shrieked. "Oh, my Gosh! How are you? We're such huge fans of yours. I mean really, huge fans. You have no idea."

"Well," said T-Bone as I hit the speaker-phone button, "we just saw your video and we can tell that you're definitely big fans. We just wanted to say thank you."

"No, thank you, boys," she replied. "I mean it, thank you. New Jersey is such an amazing place and now, thanks to you, kids are seeing what an amazing place it really is. You are creating a New Jersey Renaissance. You've made kids ask for more New Jersey; you've made it cool again."

"Wow," said T-Bone. "I had no idea. Do you think that's enough to get into the Hall of Fame?"

I reached over and slapped his head, giving him the I can't believe you just said that look that my mom is always giving me. Oddly, she answered his goofy question.

"I would absolutely put you in the Hall of Fame, I'd vote for you for Governor, and I'd put your faces all over New Jersey signs. I'd even throw you a picnic," she gushed.

"Wow," T-Bone continued, "Would you have burgers, hot dogs, and pork roll?"

"That's really not necessary," I interrupted. "We just wanted to say thank you and ask you to tell the fourth graders that we really enjoyed the video."

"You know what?" she said. "You can tell them yourselves. I'm now throwing a picnic for the fourth graders to meet you both. Maybe they'll even perform for you."

"Really?" asked T-Bone. "That's awesome. What about the hamburgers, hot dogs, and pork roll?"

"I can make hamburgers and hot dogs," she laughed. "But I don't know anything about this pork log."

"Roll," T-Bone corrected. "It's a pork roll."

"Never heard of it," she said.

"Then we'll bring some of the big rolls they make. You'll love it," he replied. "So when should we come?"

"How about Saturday?" she asked.

Before I could tell her we needed to check the calendar, T-Bone got her address and phone number.

"Well, what do you think about that?" he asked after he hung up. "It looks like we have a fan picnic to attend."

"You don't even know if we're able to get up there," I protested. "You don't even know if we're free."

"Trust me, Nick," he said with a goofy grin, "we don't have anything we couldn't move around in order to meet our fans."

T-Bone really loved saying we had fans. I preferred to think of them as New Jersey's fans. Maybe we were both right.

Chapter Three

A Little Help From Their Friends

After our amazing conversation with Mrs. Jaremack, we continued reading the suggestions and even the fan mail. I opened a large envelope from Mrs. Feldman from Alpine School in Sparta. Her students sent us amazing ideas and most of them we had never heard of. Dylan McKernan told us about the US Coast Guard Training Center in Cape May. It sounded amazing and it's the Nation's only Coast Guard Recruit Training Center. After September 11, 2001 they stopped giving individual tours, although they still offered group tours for schools and various organizations. I wondered if we could talk our teachers into a tour. Then there was Luke, another Alpine student, who suggested Waterloo Village, a 19th century restored village from a 400-year old Lenape Indian village to a bustling port along the once prosperous Morris Canal. The village is a working mill complex with gristmills and sawmills, a general store, blacksmith shop and several historic houses. I was about to put it on my list of places to visit until I checked their website. As State-owned parkland, the Village remains accessible to visitors on foot with no building access. With the exception of Canal Days, organized by the Canal Society of New Jersey and the four-day Dodge International Poetry Festival presented by the Dodge Foundation, the gates have stayed closed.

"What are you reading?" asked T-Bone.

"There's a place called Waterloo Village that sounds awesome, but it's only open a few days a year."

"Why?" he shrieked. "If it's so good, why isn't it open all of the time?"

"Probably not enough money or not enough visitors," I guessed.

"We have to get every kid in New Jersey to become history buffs," said T-Bone. "If we could get kids to see how cool looking back is, they would drag their families to check out these places and then they might be able to stay open."

"It's a good plan," I agreed, "but most kids think history's boring. I should know, I hated it more than anyone."

"Exactly," T-Bone argued. "You've just proved my point. If you, an admitted history-hater, could turn into a history buff, we can turn every kid into a buff."

"Well, I started liking history because it was cool to learn what people did and how they lived," I said. "I always wondered if I would have been able to survive like they did, without television, video games, movies, and of course, bathrooms and electricity."

"Think about it," he continued, "they built this country without the internet, cars, trains, planes, and computers. Remember, when we learned all about the Delaware & Raritan Canal and how they dug it by hand? Or the Howell Farm still uses tools from long ago?"

"You know," I agreed, "you're right. With all of the advantages we have, shouldn't we be doing amazing things? If all those past generations could accomplish so much with so little, we should be able to solve big problems and come up with big ideas. We can communicate instantly, we can find anything out the moment we wonder about it, and we hardly wait for anything. Don't we have a responsibility to do big things?"

"Wow, if you were standing at a podium on a stage right now, that would have been a great speech," T-Bone laughed.

"Unless there were people in the audience," I reminded him. "Then I would have sounded like I had carmel and marbles in my mouth."

As we continued through the piles, we came across Katie Hannan, also from Mrs. Feldman's class. She suggested the Schoolhouse Museum in Paramus. According to Katie, on the Old Paramus Reformed Church campus is the one-room, church-like schoolhouse. The building now houses the Ridgewood Historical and Preservation Society and is known as The Schoolhouse Museum. It was built in 1872 and was used as a school until 1905. Morgan Wrigley from the Hillside school in Mount Laurel wrote about the Abbott Farm in Hamilton Township, Mercer County. It's a National Historic Landmark and was known as the largest Middle

Woodland Village of its type on the Eastern Seaboard. It's recognized as one of the nation's most important archeological sites. I wondered how many people that didn't live in those towns actually knew about those places. Then I wondered if everyone who lived in those towns actually knew about them.

We also came across a letter from Lance LaPorte, from Ridgeway School, in Toms River. He told us about Cattus Island on the Barnegat Bay in his town. The main trail leads to the woods, a marsh and then to a glistening beach. He even told us about the Cooper Environmental Center and how the naturalists give talks on weekends.

"You know what these kids are telling us?" I asked.

"Yeah," T-Bone shrugged and sighed. "They're telling us where we should visit."

"No," I replied. "They're telling us that we still have so much more to explore in New Jersey. Even as we wait for our Official Junior Ambassador bill to be passed, we're still finding new places."

"That's okay," T-Bone said with a new level of confidence. "It doesn't matter what we know, it's more important that we're still exploring. And even more important than that is now everybody else is exploring and thinking about New Jersey. It's win-win."

When he had a point, he had a point. I asked my mom if we could go to Rockaway on Saturday and told her why. As much as she wanted to meet the creative minds behind our song and dance, she already had other plans and my dad was working. We knew exactly who to call and my grandfather was happy to take us. My grandmother told me that we were keeping him young and I told her he was making us smarter. It seemed like a fair trade.

"Hey, I have a good one," T-Bone said as he held a sheet of paper in the air. "It's from Zak Van Es, also from Mrs. Feldman's class. He said we should tell everyone about the USS Ling 297."

"What's a USS Ling?" I asked.

"USS Ling 297," T-Bone corrected.

"Okay," I sighed, "what's a USS Ling 297?"

"I'm glad you asked," he said. "The New Jersey Naval Museum's star attraction is the USS Ling (SS297), an interactive Memorial to the Veterans of all branches of the United States armed forces who fought for, and died for, our Liberty and Freedom."

"The museum sounds great, but you still haven't told me what a Ling is."

"You mean a USS Ling 297," he repeated.

"Just tell me," I demanded.

"The museum offers visitors the opportunity to view rare historic equipment and artifacts, photographs and other memorabilia. It also honors New Jersey's role in the war and includes a shrine to the 3,505 men who made the supreme sacrifice in defense of their country in World War II. The museum has served as an educational facility for schools, Scout troops and other organizations."

"Okay, for the last time, what is a USS Ling 297?"

"Oh, it's a submarine," he said matter-of-factly. "The USS LING 297 is a BALAO class fleet submarine. It's 312 feet long, weighing about 2,500 tons and permanently berthed in Hackensack, New Jersey."

"That's cool," I nodded. "Hackensack has a naval museum and a submarine?"

"But it needs help," said T-Bone.

"Let me guess," I said. "No money and no visitors, so it's only open a couple of days a week?"

"Even worse," T-Bone explained, "the people who own the land want to develop the property and they want the museum and Ling moved."

"That's terrible," I said, becoming very angry. "It's bad enough people insisted on moving Lucy the Elephant, but how do you move a whole museum and a submarine?"

"You're right," he shook his head, "I forgot about poor Lucy being moved after people wanted to demolish her. Wasn't it a judge who heard the case on a weekend that saved Lucy? Maybe we can find that judge."

"I don't think it works that way," I shrugged.

We went on their website and read about how the Ling needed help. It said they need our support to keep the World War II submarine, USS Ling, in Hackensack, N.J. We decided Zak wasn't only helping kids learn about World War II and New Jersey's role in our country's freedom, he was also honoring veterans. Since veterans always keep us safe and protected, we figured we owed them one. We decided to write a special report about it for the state website.

"Look at this," I said, holding up a paper from yet another student in Mrs. Feldman's class, Rebecca Greenberg.

"Wow," T-Bone shook his head. "Just how big is Mrs. Feldman's class?"

"I don't know, but Rebecca wrote about another really interesting place called the Liberty Hall Museum."

"Does it have a bell?" asked T-Bone.

"What do you mean?" I asked.

"Does it have a bell with a long, giant crack in it?" he continued. "Isn't there a bell with a giant crack because they rang it too hard calling the soldiers in for dinner?"

"What?" I laughed. "Are you talking about the Liberty Bell in Philadelphia?"

"Was that one used as a dinner bell, too?"

"No, it wasn't a dinner bell. Haven't you ever been to Philly? How do you not know about the Liberty Bell?"

"Maybe because I didn't live next to it, like you did," he tried to defend himself.

"You don't have to live near it to know about it," I laughed. "You know what? We're gonna do a special trip to Philly. I'll show you the Liberty Bell, the Constitution Center, the Comcast building, and the Art Museum steps."

"Steps? Why would I want to look at steps?" T-Bone laughed. "Wow, no wonder they never asked you to be the Official Ambassador for Pennsylvania. You'd be a terrible tour guide. I could just see it. Now, folks if you look to your left you will see a telephone pole, on the right is a house, and oh, look up ahead, there are the steps."

"You've really never heard of the Art Museum Steps?" I asked in disbelief. It wasn't like T-Bone lived on the moon or in Morocco. I assumed everyone knew about the Art Museum steps.

"Why would I have heard about steps?" he smugly replied. "Do they do tricks? Did George Washington give a speech on them? Do they sing?"

"Haven't you ever seen the Rocky movies?"

  looking into the eye of the tiger," he said, pointing to his eye and furrowing his eyebrow. "Of course, I've seen the Rocky movies."

"Do you remember when he runs up the steps?"

"Who doesn't remem...wait a minute, are those the Rocky steps?" he jumped up and pretended to run in slow motion. "Those steps have a name? I thought they were the Rocky steps. I didn't know they were real. You have to bring me to Philly."

"Okay, Rocky," I laughed, "but let's work on one project at a time. Let's keep going through the piles."

"Hey, these two are both from Mrs. Feldman's class. One's from Olivia Cella and the other is from Delaney Sniffen," T-Bone said holding up two sheets of paper. "And they both think we should visit a place called Sterling Hill Mine."

"A coal mine?" I asked.

"No, it's a zinc mine," said T-Bone.

I took a look at their suggestions and, once again, I learned about a place I had never heard of that was right here in New Jersey. The mine sounded awesome so I checked out the website. There was a link on Trip Advisor and everyone gave this place great reviews. They had black lights inside so visitors could see the rocks glow in the dark. I wondered how a rock could glow if it wasn't painted, but it turned out that they were actually phosphorescent. I had never ever heard of Ogdensburg, New Jersey so I went to Google Maps and there it was. Ironically, it wasn't much farther than Rockaway and the Hibernia Diner.

"Hey, T-Bone," I began, "do you think we should take the 11:00 am tour that they have on Saturday and then meeting the Rockaway kids after that?"

"A zinc mine and a picnic with our fans?" he smiled. "Sounds like a good day to me. Maybe we could have breakfast at the Hibernia Diner since we'll be in the mine during lunch."

T-Bone was the only person I knew who always worried about eating lunch at noon and dinner at five. Since we became ambassadors he had become a little more flexible, as long as he had a Plan B. As we continued sorting out the suggestions and letters we came across a really interesting suggestion from a girl named Aniah Wilson from the John Glen School in Pine Hill, New Jersey.

She wrote about her town and an amusement park with a water park. T-Bone was very interested in visiting Pine Hill and Clementon Park.

"Is it near Rockaway?" he asked. "If it is, maybe we can go there on the same day?"

"You want to drive almost two hours, have breakfast at the Hibernia Diner, tour the Sterling Hill Mine, go to a fan picnic, and then visit another town and amusement park in one day?" I asked.

"And the water park," he said. "Don't forget the water park."

"Then don't forget the helicopter," I laughed as I looked at Google Maps, "because Pine Hill is in south Jersey."

"Too much?" he asked.

"Uh, just a little," I sarcastically answered.

"Okay," he said, "but I still want to check it out. Aniah wrote about the historic Tomlinson House, too. Let's put it on the list."

"Done," I said as I added it to our must-see column.

"Hey, listen to this one," T-Bone began. It's from Alexi Garcia and he suggests we visit New Brunswick."

"Where in New Brunswick?" I asked, assuming Alexi must have written about a water park.

"That's what's so cool," he explained. "He wrote about the entire city. You know Rutgers University is in New Brunswick and they have a ton of restaurants. He also said they have theaters like the State Theater and the George Street Theater."

"So far so good," I said, definitely interested in exploring an entire town. I read Alexi's suggestions and decided his idea would go on the top of our list. "Since New Brunswick is a whole town, maybe we should invite Alexi to come with us."

"Good idea," T-Bone agreed. "Put New Brunswick, the Sterling Hill Mine, and Pine Hill on our list."

"Done," I said as I closed my notebook. "Although, we won't visit them in that order since we're going to visit the Sterling Hill Mine and the Rockaway kids on Saturday."

"Wrong," said T-Bone. "We'll be visiting our Rockaway fans on Saturday!"

Chapter Four

Sterling HIll Mine & Rockaway Kids

"Nicky," my mom said as she opened my bedroom door. "What time are you leaving for Rockaway and the mine?"

"Pop said he would be here at eight o'clock," I answered.

"Okay, well you better get up now," she said.

I looked at the clock and noticed it was only 6:30 a.m. and realized there was only one reason my mom would wake me up an hour and a half early.

"Is T-Bone downstairs?" I asked.

"He sure is," she smiled. "Get ready and I'll send him up."

Luckily, my mom answered the door and she had a soft spot for T-Bone. If my dad answered, he might have left him sitting on the porch for a while. While my mom entertained him, I took a quick shower. I ran downstairs and quickly stopped when T-Bone turned around. He was wearing a suit and dark sunglasses. He had his hair slicked to the side and I noticed a NJ pin on his lapel.

"What are you doing?" I asked as I rubbed my eyes.

"Touring a mine and meeting my fans,"he shrugged. "You're not wearing that are you?"

I was wearing shorts, a t-shirt, sneakers, and a baseball hat. "You realize we're going to a mine and a picnic, don't you?"

"We're touring a mine," he corrected.

"Everybody that visits Sterling Hill is touring a mine," I tried to explain. "I think you should go home and get changed."

"No way," he protested. "I need to make a really

good impression on my fans. Plus, Mr. Campaign Manager, have you forgotten something important?"

"My top hat?" I laughed.

"No, we'll be around other kids and other kids vote," he said. "That's why I'm wearing a New Jersey pin on my label."

"Tommy,"my mom interrupted, "it's actually called a lapel and only the kids in your school can vote for you."

"Really?" he asked, sinking into the couch. "My Rockaway fans can't vote for me? Maybe I should go home and change."

"Sorry," she smiled. "But if it makes you feel better, I think you look very handsome. You may be a little over-dressed for a mine and a picnic, but you do look very, very presidential."

"Really?" he asked, perking back up. "You really think I look very presidential? Cool, I'm gonna keep my suit on."

"Why?" I asked. "These kids can't vote for you."

"Nick, Nick, Nick," he shook his head. "If I'm

running for office, I should always look presidential. I'm gonna wear a suit every day."

"Thanks, Mom," I said as I turned to look at her. "You've been a major help."

"Sorry," she whispered as she went back upstairs.

My grandfather arrived with a cooler of Case's pork roll, took one look at T-Bone and didn't say a word. He just smiled. He had spent enough time with him and knew better than to ask questions.

Our first stop would be the Hibernia Diner. It was a long drive, but it was really interesting. For such a small state, New Jersey had an amazing, always changing landscape. One moment, we were on the busy turnpike, heading toward the almost as busy Route 287. But something strange happens on Route 287. The farther north you drive, the more the landscape rises. Suddenly, the trees that line highway morph into mountains. The mountains of North Jersey were so different from the flat farmlands of south Jersey, the Pine Barrens along the coast, and the busy cities. These differences were one of the things that made New Jersey so awesome; plus, the fact that you could see any of these places on a tank of gas definitely helped.

When we arrived at the Hibernia Diner, we were met by George, one of the owners. When T-Bone told him who we were, he smiled and thanked us for writing about the diner in our reports. T-Bone was still wearing his sunglasses and as I stared at him across the table, I noticed they were huge. I hadn't realized it earlier because I was so distracted by the suit, the teeth, and the hair, but there was something strange about them.

"Where did you get those glasses?" I asked, as plates piled high with pancakes and eggs were delivered.

"On the kitchen table; they're my dad's glasses," he said as he lowered them and looked at me over the top. "They make me look like a rock star, huh?"

"I don't think so," I laughed. "I think remember your mom wearing those glasses."

"Really?" he asked, definitely not concerned that he was wearing ladies glasses.

While my grandfather finished his second cup of coffee and got directions from George, T-Bone and I looked over our notes about the mine.

The drive to the mine was pretty quick and when

we pulled into the parking lot, I tried to imagine what it would feel like to be in a mine. We headed to the museum building first and there were two statues in front. On the left was a statue of two miners with a large piece of equipment.

"What do you think that is?" I asked my grandfather, pointing to the large tool.

"Actually," said a man standing behind us, "that's a stamp mill."

"Wow, that's pretty good," I said, definitely impressed with his knowledge of mines. "I guess you've been here before?"

"See those handsome miners," he said, pointing to the statue. "Do they look familiar?"

"No," said T-Bone.

He grabbed the man he had been speaking with, and they each stood next to a statue. We didn't get it at first, but my grandfather did and he started laughing. A few seconds later, I got it, too.

"Hey," I asked, "are those really statues of you guys?"

"I'm the handsome one," said the other man.

"Are you real miners?" asked T-Bone.

"No, just real handsome," laughed the first man.

"Hi, folks, I'm Richard Hauck and this is my brother, Bob. We purchased the mine in 1989."

"Wow, did you become millionaires?" T-Bone gushed.

"Millionaires?" they asked.

"Sure," T-Bone explained, "if you own the mine, you get to keep all of the diamonds, rubies, and gold."

"Diamonds, rubies, and gold?" asked a younger man who had just left the building. "Sign me up."

"Are you a real miner?" asked T-Bone.

"No, sir, my name is Robert Hauck," he said extending his hand. "I guess you've met my dad and my Uncle Richard."

"We did," I answered as I shook his hand. "Is that a statue of you?"

"I'd like to say yes, but that's actually a miner looking at a canary in his hand."

"Cool," said T-Bone, "but what about the diamonds, rubies, and gold?"

"Well," Uncle Richard started, "I guess we'd be rich if this was a diamond, ruby, or gold mine, but this mine is famous for its zinc ore with a very, very high concentration of minerals that glow under ultraviolet light."

"Wow," T-Bone shrieked. "Cool. Zinc ore that glows in the dark is very cool. Hey, what's zinc ore?"

"You'll find out on your tour," Bob smiled. "This is your first time visiting us?"

"Yes, sir," I replied, "but we checked out your website and we're really excited."

"We're actually New Jersey's soon-to-be Official Junior Ambassadors," T-Bone explained. "We visit places all over the state and write reports for the state's website. We didn't even know about your mine until two girls from Sparta wrote us a letter."

"Amazing," said Robert. "Do you know their names?"

"Sure," I said, "it's Olivia Cella and Delaney Sniffen. Do you know them?"

"No," he smiled, "but we should thank them for sending you our way. Have you ever toured a mine?"

"No," I answered. "And I usually think of coal when I think of mines. I never realized there were mines with minerals."

"Well, I'll give you a little heads up," said Robert. "My uncle here discovered an unknown mineral."

"Are you famous?" I asked.

"Not exactly," he smiled, "but there is now a mineral called Hauckite. Who knows, maybe I'm famous to fans of minerals.

"Minerals wouldn't happen to be historical, would they?" asked T-Bone.

"Well, they're very old and give us clues and answers about the past that help us understand the present and future," explained Bob.

"Then I'm a fan," said T-Bone, excited to make a history connection. "So, what's on the tour?"

"You'll start in the Zobel Exhibit Hall where you'll see amazing displays that include lockers, fossils, a periodic table of elements display, and some minerals that glow. For many of our visitors the most exciting part of the tour is the Rainbow Room, where fluorescent zinc ore is exposed in the mine walls, exactly as it was in other parts of the mine where ore was produced. Illuminated under ultraviolet light, the walls glow green and red."

"Green and red?" T-Bone grasped. "How can they glow green and red? Did they paint them with glow-in-the-dark paint?"

"No," Robert laughed, "the green signals the presence of Willemite, one of the main zinc ore minerals at Sterling Hill. There's also Franklinite and Zincite. "

"That sounds awesome," I said. "But we get to go into a real mine, right? It's not one of those fake mines or a re-creation of a mine, is it?"

"Oh, it's real," Richard laughed. "A 1,300-ft underground stroll through the mine is a featured part of the tour. Within the mine passages you'll see numerous pieces of equipment used while the mine was in operation, plus exhibits on the underground mining process. He told us we'd also see the lamp room, the shaft station, mine galleries dating to the 1830's, and much more.

When we walked into the gift shop to buy our tickets, I noticed the how many rocks and minerals were for sale. T-Bone, of course, noticed the Miners Lunchbox, the lunch counter and snack bar. As we waited to start the tour, the size of the crowd started growing. They led us past some more statues, coal cars, and a railroad crossing sign. There was even a tombstone for a cat named Princess Sterling. We started in the Zobel Exhibit Hall and our tour guide, Ray, stopped at the lockers. We spotted clothes, boots, and lunchboxes hanging from the ceiling. We learned that when the miners left the mine, they were filthy and soaking wet so they hung everything up to dry. Then we learned that the mine was always 56 degrees. There were pictures of miners and they didn't look very happy.

"Hey, T-Bone, it's always 56 degrees in the mine and they were always soaking wet," I whispered. "No wonder the statues and pictures look so serious."

"You don't think my suit'll get wet, do you?" he asked.

"I don't know," I shrugged. "Let me find a picture of a miner in a suit and I'll see if it looks wet."

"Good idea," he said, examining the old black and white pictures on the wall. I wondered how long it would take him to realize miners didn't wear suits in the mine.

Luckily, he was distracted by a large fossil of a dinosaur head. Then he pointed to the sign that named the five things we must find before the tour. It was the most interesting scavenger hunt I could remember. When we headed to the rainbow room, everyone on the tour was very excited. We looked at rocks that looked like any other rocks. That is, until they turned off the regular light and turned on the black light. Suddenly, the room was aglow; so were T-Bone's ultra-white teeth. While everyone's teeth were glowing, looking at T-Bone was like looking at the sun.

Everyone started to ooh and ahh so much that it felt like we were at a fireworks show. T-Bone was right, I couldn't believe they didn't paint the rocks with glow-in-the-dark paint. By the time we entered the mine, Ray, our tour guide, had every person spellbound. As we walked through the entrance, he pointed out a picture of real miners, walking through the same entrance. A chill ran down my spine. They probably never imagined the mine they worked in would one day be preserved for tourists.

Inside, it was a lot cleaner than I expected. It was also cold. They said it would be 56 degrees and they weren't kidding. I felt bad about the miners working in this temperature while they were wet. My grandfather and I threw on our sweatshirts and T-Bone, who was sweating all day, finally had some relief.

As we followed the passages, they had displays set up with mannequin miners so we could really understand what they did inside. It was definitely hard work and Ray told us that every year, about two men died. When they drilled the mine, in 1840, they did it by hand and were only able to drill one foot each day. It reminded me of the immigrants digging the Delaware & Raritan Canal.

As the tour ended, we saw Robert and he asked us if we enjoyed our first mine. When we told him we definitely enjoyed it, he smiled. I asked him about the pictures of Thomas Edison I had noticed in Zobel Hall and he explained that Thomas Edison founded the Edison Iron Mine in 1890 and invented many things used in mining.

"Really?" asked T-Bone. "Are you talking about the same Thomas Edison that invented everything else? The same Thomas Edison that was in the 2008 Inaugural Class of the Hall of Fame? Light bulb Thomas Edison?"

"That's the one," Robert smiled. "He was a very talented gentleman, that's for sure."

"I'm just wondering if that guy ever slept," T-Bone shook his head, "and how he got so smart."

"Well, you could always visit his laboratory in West Orange, New Jersey or his mansion to find out more about him," suggested Richard.

"Nick, write that down," he said as if he was my boss. I started thinking the suit was going to his head.

As usual, one New Jersey location gave us an idea for another and the Thomas Edison connection did just that. I opened my notebook and made a note that we needed to learn more about Thomas Edison and his lab. Actually, we needed to know about his life. We waved good-bye to the Haucks and headed south.

T-Bone was really excited to go to Mrs. Jaremack's house and even though I tried to act cool about it, I was pretty excited, too. When we arrived, there were balloons and welcome signs staked in the grass. As we started walking toward the house,

the kids ran out front, assembled into their forma-
tion and started singing. It was even better in real
life. When they finished, T-Bone started it again
and jumped in the line. Everyone was laughing,
probably at the guy with the brown face, white
neck, and lady glasses wearing a suit. Or maybe it
was at his dancing.

Everyone was awesome. We met the teachers, Mrs.
Jaremack, Mrs. Beck, and Mrs. Frauenpreis as
well as the technology teacher, Mrs. O'Donnel, who
served as their filmmaker. While Mr. Jaremack
was at the grill, we presented him with one of
Trenton's treasures, two long rolls of pork roll.
Some people called it Taylor ham, some people had
never even heard of it, but these kids were in for a
Trenton treat.

T-Bone thought it would be a good idea to mingle,
so that's what we did. Even though they couldn't
vote for him, T-Bone wanted to know all about
them. Of course, he started by asking every kid
about their favorite place in New Jersey. I thought
their answers were interesting. Owen Tanis,
Nicole Knorr, Amanda Perez, Nicholas Angelillo,
Cameron Harrington, Brock Nienhouse, Russel
Cuny, and Tairah Mandes all picked Green Pond.
Madison Vandermark picked Mt. Hope Pond,
Matthew Strina picked the Ford Fasche House,

and Natalie Napolitano and Skylar Walder both picked Rockaway. It was nice that they really loved where they lived. I was curious where the other kids loved to visit and they had some amazing ideas. Dan and Ben Philhower and Kenny Ruch told us all about the Sterling Hill Mine and T-Bone and I started laughing.

"You just came back from the mine?" Ben and Dan said at the same time.

"We just left," T-Bone announced proudly. "Why?"

"You just seem a little overdressed," they laughed.

"Presidential, huh?" T-Bone winked.

As they continued to tell us their favorite places, I felt pretty proud. We had written reports about many of them, which means we had a good sense of what kids like. That, of course, was probably because we were kids. Ethan Bockholm loved Long Beach Island and we talked about Bill Burr's Flamingo golf. Stephanie Schlemmer picked Lucy the Elephant and Ashley George and Ava Schneider both picked Atlantic City.

"Did you look out Lucy's giant glass eye and see what she sees?"asked T-Bone.

"Of course," she smiled. "Did you see her rib?"

"I have a picture of it in my wallet," he laughed.

The funny part was, he probably did.

When we started talking about how great the Jersey Shore was, Alyssa Scafa and Sage Napolitano told us how they loved the Wildwoods. T-Bone agreed and reminded them to wear shoes when walking on the hot sand. The beaches at Wildwood aren't only free, they're extremely wide and T-Bone would know. The last time we went, he hopped all the way to the ocean, screaming about his feet burning.

Edward Haag told us about how much he loved the Camden Aquarium and we told him how we take New Jersey Transit's River Line Train to get there. He thought that was pretty cool. Joey Yosco talked about Jockey Hollow, one of my favorite places. When we visited the Ford Mansion and Jockey Hollow it felt like the soldiers were still there. One of the most interesting ideas came from Edison Scherr. He suggested we visit Thomas Edison's Lab in Menlo Park and we told him that we just learned about some more of Thomas Edison's work with mines at Sterling Hill.

"You know," said Edison, "that's who I'm named after."

"You're named after a Mr. Scherr?" a confused T-Bone asked.

"No, Einstein, his name is Edison," I said.

"Your name is Edison Einstein?" asked T-Bone.

"No, I was calling you Einstein. His name is Edison. He's named after Thomas Edison," I tried once more.

"Okay, if you're Edison, who's Mr. Scherr?" he asked with impatient frustration.

Thankfully, Mr. Jaremack announced that the food was ready. Rather than explain once more, it was easier to put a pork roll and cheese sandwich in his hand. Luckily, that did the trick. While my grandfather spoke with the teachers, all of the kids were so busy eating that the yard was silent. We sat in the shade and spoke with Eddie, Matt, Nathan, Ashley and Katie. Before long, most of the kids were surrounding T-Bone. Maybe it was the suit and hair, but I knew the real reason people gravitated to him. T-Bone was a people person and he loved talking and learning about others. For a moment there, he actually looked like a politician.

Before long, he was talking politics. I went to grab a bottle of water and came back to hear T-Bone listening to their ideas. He must have asked them what they would do if they were Governor. Some of the ideas were very creative. I liked Brock's idea of putting an indoor pool in his room and Kenny's idea of making everything free. Some of the ideas were very generous. Nicholas would make sure every community was safe, Sage wanted to make sure everyone had a home so no one would be homeless, and Nicole wanted everyone to have a job.

Two ideas caught T-Bone's attention. Stephanie said encourage families to visit New Jersey and Matthew said New Jersey should finally make us official. Suddenly, from behind a bunch of kids, a voice said, "I would get rid of some of the politicians." It was Natalie and as soon as she said it, T-Bone froze.

"Huh?" he asked.

"I think we should get rid of politicians who don't do their jobs," she said.

"But we need politicians for government," said T-Bone.

"No," she corrected. "We need politicians who do

their job to have a good government."

"She has a good point," I laughed. "Plus, she didn't say, all, she said some politicians. And I guarantee you that every good politician would agree."

"You guys," T-Bone addressed the whole group, "I want to be a politician."

The yard was silent and he wasn't sure what they would say. I wasn't sure what they would say. Then they said, "Cool." They nodded their heads and seemed to think it was great. I decided to change the subject and we started naming our favorite New Jerseyans. As predicted, so many kids picked obvious choices: Bruce Springsteen, Jon Bon Jovi, Derek Jeter, Neal Armstrong, and Buddy "The Cake Boss" Valastro. But then there were several kids who picked Thomas Alva Edison. I thought I knew about Edison, but the more they told me, the more I needed to learn.

Soon Mrs. Jaremack brought out cupcakes, Mrs. Beck brought out ice cream, Mrs. Frauenpreis brought out brownies, and Mrs. O'Donnel brought out cookies. T-Bone, of course, suddenly forgot about politics and New Jersey. He was the first person in line. When everyone had their dessert, Mrs. Jaremack stood up to make a toast.

"Nicky, T-Bone, Pop," she smiled, "we are so happy to have the opportunity to meet you and to tell you how much we appreciate your work. You have inspired so many people to explore this most wonderful state we live in and we all thank you."

With that everyone raised their juices and took a sip. Before I could swallow, I saw T-Bone stand up and walk toward Mrs. Jaremack. Please sit down, I thought. Just please sit down. Of course, I knew he wasn't going to sit down.

"I don't know what to say," he began. "Nicky and I have been working very hard to be good junior ambassadors. Whether it's unofficial or official, it doesn't really matter. Well, actually, it kind of does matter. I mean, I know politics move slow, but really, we should be official by now. I mean, we spend so much time researching places and then dragging Pop and Mr. and Mrs. A. all over the state. And don't even get me started on the reports and pictures for the website."

"I think what he means," I interrupted, trying to change the subject, "is that we really think the song and dance are very cool and we cannot believe you did that for us. So thank you."

Poor T-Bone was standing there, sweating in his

suit, with his hair starting to get puffy from the humidity. He didn't bring it up much, but he must have been really upset that we weren't official yet. I guess I hadn't noticed how upset he was. For me, sharing New Jersey was enough. After moving here, I realized what an awesome state it was and I enjoyed making sure other people knew that, too. But, for T-Bone, it was more. He wanted more. But he didn't want the title of Official Junior Ambassador just to have it or just to tell people about it. He wanted the title because he believed it would make a difference. I felt really bad that he was so upset about the delay and wished I could make the vote happen quicker. T-Bone's speech was really about his frustration with how long it can take ideas, especially good ones, to be enacted.

Luckily, before T-Bone could continue, Mrs. Jaremack extended her toast..

"T-Bone, Nicky, I don't think anyone, in the history of New Jersey, has been as interested in getting people excited about our state," she said with a huge smile.

"I agree," Mrs. Beck nodded. "You're kids, you don't get paid, and you still devote so much time to New Jersey. I have no doubt that you'll get your vote."

"What if they don't vote yes?" he asked, realizing for the first time that even when it went for a vote, it wasn't guaranteed. "What if they schedule our bill for a vote and then they all vote no?"

Mrs. Frauenpreis laughed. "Why would they vote no? Teachers and parents depend upon your reports to know where to bring their families. I happen to think you're great for the state! "

And, my grandfather smiled as he patted T-Bone's fluffy hair, "Let's not forget the most important thing... *you're free.*"

Chapter Five

New Brunswick

Only two days had passed since our trip to the Sterling Hill Mine and Rockaway. As soon as we finished our report we started planning for our next adventure. We decided to take Alexi Garcia's advice and check out the City of New Brunswick. We remembered touring the City of Burlington, with some help from the Mayor and wondered if we should call New Brunswick's City Hall. We also agreed that T-Bone should make that call.

A few minutes later, he hung up and said we had an appointment the next day with two gentlemen, Russell and Michael from the Mayor's office. I knew my parents weren't available and decided to see if my grandfather was up for another trip so quickly. Before I could finish, he asked me what time we needed him there. Maybe my grandmother was right and we were keeping him young.

There wasn't much time to prepare for this trip, so it was nice that we would have tour guides. The next morning T-Bone arrived bright and early, as usual. I was hoping he wouldn't be wearing his suit and thankfully, he wasn't. Unfortunately, his face looked a couple of shades darker than before.

"Hey, what happened to wearing your suit all of the time," I asked.

"My mom said she has no intention of letting me wear my good suit everyday and no intention of buying me more suits," he explained. "You don't have an extra suit I could borrow, do you?"

After pretending to think about it, I told him no. I doubted my mom wanted T-Bone wearing my only good suit every other day. We went downstairs and found my grandfather having coffee with my parents.

"You boys all set?" he asked.

"Yeah," I answered. "I have my map, my notebook, the camera, and a bunch of printouts from New Brunswick's website."

We headed north on the New Jersey Turnpike and got off on exit 9. There were several busy highways, like Route 1 and Route 18, and a lot of traffic. Luckily, my grandfather was a good driver.

Our first stop was City Hall where we went into a conference room with Russell and Michael. They were really friendly and gave us firm handshakes. As we sat down, they handed us some maps and brochures. We showed them the letter that Alexi had written and they also wanted to meet him.

"T-Bone said you both enjoy history," said Russell.

"Very much," I said, trying to sound less like a kid and more like an adult.

"Then you'll love our city. New Brunswick is a where old meets new. Take this building we're sitting in; it was built in 1927, but it has everything we need to run a modern city. And we're also home to Rutgers University, the second oldest university in New Jersey and the eighth oldest university in the United States."

"Do you have any historic houses?" asked T-Bone.

"Yes, but rather than sit in an office and tell about what we have, we'll show you?" Michael suggested.

"I have a van downstairs that's ready to go."

"Could we bring Alexi Garcia with us?" asked T-Bone, as everyone turned in surprise.

"How do you even know if he's home?" I asked.

"I didn't tell you this before, but I told him to meet us at City Hall," T-Bone explained. "Surprise!"

"Is he here?" I asked.

"He should be here any minute," T-Bone smiled.

I had no idea that T-Bone had arranged for Alexi to spend the day with us and I thought it was a great idea. Now that we had Alexi, Michael, and Russell, we would definitely learn everything we needed to know about the City of New Brunswick.

When we opened the door to the back parking lot, Alexi, who was 11 years old, was standing there with his sister, Yurilian, who was 13. He had a big smile and we were happy to meet them both. As we piled into the van, it was exciting. We were meeting new people and a new city at the same time. Everything was going great and then T-Bone asked Alexi what his favorite shows were. When he said Cake Boss, T-Bone nearly hit the floor.

Poor Alexi had no idea how excited T-Bone would become. He told him about how we met the family and went to the bakery and even told him how Buddy's niece, Tessy and her mom, Lisa, are great friends of his. I had no idea what Alexi was thinking, because T-Bone never let him get a word in, but he kept smiling.

As we drove past the post office and the police headquarters, we saw a giant sculpture of an animal. T-Bone thought it was a reindeer, but Russell pointed out that it was an elk. This made sense, since it was in front of the Elks Lodge. We drove past the Henry Guest House and learned that in 1755, Businessman Henry Guest bought land on what is now Livingston Avenue and New Street. Five years later, he built a sturdy house, with thick stone walls and a solid foundation. He was sure it would last through storms and time. He was right. Even after moving it 250 feet, it was in great shape.

"I'd take you in, but they're working," said Russell.

"What are they doing?" I asked.

"They're making a library annex for meetings and exhibits," he explained. "It's said that this is the best stone house in the state."

As we passed by, I knew they were right. A moment later, we pulled over in front of the Willow Grove Cemetery. They pointed to columns in the back and explained that one of the most unusual areas of the cemetery was the Japanese Section. It was purchased in 1870 by Rutgers College as a burial plot for the Japanese exchange student Kusakabe Taro. This plot became the final resting place for eight citizens of Japan who were studying or working in the Tri-State area. Every year, New Brunswick hosts a ceremony at this plot in remembrance of the deceased students as part of its involvement with its Sister Cities in Japan.

"Wow," T-Bone gasped, "New Brunswick has sister cities in Japan. That's cool."

"Very cool," Alexi agreed, "I didn't even know that." This tour was great, I thought. Even Alexi was learning more about where he lived. We drove through the Rutgers campus and it was exactly how I pictured a college town. The buildings were huge and old, but not bad old. They were that really cool kind of old. As we approached a river, T-Bone asked if it was the Delaware River. Before anyone could say a word, Alexi answered.

"That's the Raritan River," he said. "And this is Boyd Park where we have a playground, fireworks, a boat landing, and an amphitheatre. It's named after Elmer Boyd, the former publisher of the Home News."

"Well, somebody did their homework," Michael smiled. "Where'd you learn all of that?"

"Ms. Rosa, my fourth grade teacher, told us all about New Brunswick," he smiled proudly. "And also Mrs. Youseff."

"Are they your favorite teachers?" I asked.

"Yes," he hesitated, "but then I'd have to add Mrs. Palfey from first grade, too. I don't think she taught me about New Brunswick, but she was also one of my favorite teachers."

As we walked through the park, we saw something very familiar; it was the Delaware & Raritan Canal. T-Bone looked like he just found a long, lost friend. When Russell pointed out the locks, T-Bone was confused and asked how a city could lock up a whole canal and why they would want to.

"No, no," Russell smiled. "The locks are sections of the canal that were used to overcome differences in elevation."

T-Bone still looked confused until Russell explained that if one part of the canal was higher than another part, the locks could allow boats to get to the higher or lower section. A boat heading downstream would enter the lock, the gates would close, the downstream gates would open and the boat would be lowered. Once the water levels on each side were equal, the downstream gates would open and the boat could keep going. To go upstream, they just did it in reverse.

"Why didn't they just make it all the same height when they built it?" I asked.

"That's a good question," said Michael. "You see, when they built the canal, they had to follow the land. Since land has different elevations, canals do, too."

When we left the park, we headed to Route 27, which is also called the Lincoln Highway. We learned that it was the first transcontinental highway in the United States and people used it to drive from New Jersey to California. Another first, right here in New Jersey, I thought.Our route took us past a giant Hyatt Hotel, the Johnson and Johnson Tower, which used to be the city's tallest building, the Old Bay restaurant and several very old churches.

"Hey, Alexi, do you want to go to Rutgers when you grow up?" asked T-Bone.

"Maybe," he said. "But I don't know if you need to go to college for the jobs I want to do."

"What do you want to be?" asked my grandfather.

"Well, my first choice would be lumberjack and if I can't do that, I'd like to be in NASCAR."

"A NASCAR driver is really cool," said T-Bone. "If I hadn't already decided to be a politician, a pulmonologist, and a member of the Hall of Fame, I might add that to my list."

"First," I interrupted, "how many times have you rode your bike into street signs?"

"Six," said T-Bone "If you don't count stop signs."

"I'd count them," I nodded.

"Okay, sixteen," he admitted. "But in my defense, I think the sidewalks have gotten skinnier or the bikes have gotten wider. Something's not right."

"And, second," I continued, "for the gazillionth time, it's a philanthropist. The word you're always

86

looking for, the word that means a person who gives money away to good causes, is philanthropist."

"Guys," Alexi laughed, "I don't want to be a driver; it looks dangerous. I'd rather be in the pit crew. That looks exciting."

"That's different," I laughed. "Most kids always want to be the driver. I like when people think differently. How about you, Yurilian?"

"I'd like to be a pediatrician," she said softly. "I might even go to Rutgers."

"That's awesome," I told her. "I'm thinking about starting a business, but I don't know what kind. Maybe I'll go to Rutgers for business. Maybe I'll see you there; maybe by the Grease Trucks."

"You know Rutgers was founded in 1766 and was called the Queens campus," Michael saved me before I said the word maybe once more. "If you visit the Geology Museum, you can even see the Wooly Mammoth. And if you visit the university in April for the Rutgers Day festival, you can really see all they have to offer."

"Can anyone go?" asked T-Bone.

"Yes, absolutely," Russell smiled. "There's usually about 75,000 students, alumni, and visitors each year. It's an amazing event."

Before T-Bone could tell me, I made a note about it in my book. Our next stop was Buccleuch Park. They told us that the locals pronounced it *bugle-o*. It was huge, with a pavilion, gazebo, playground, tennis courts, athletic fields, a rock garden and Red Barn Hill. This city was so cool, that in the winter, on snowy days, they would close the road and let kids sled down the hill.

"That's my kind of Mayor," I said, nodding my head.

"Speaking of the Mayor," said Russell. "Alexi, do you know who the Mayor is?"

"Yes, sir," Alexi replied with a grin, "everybody knows that; it's Mayor Cahill. He's been the Mayor for a long time."

"Over twenty years," said Michael, as T-Bone's eyes glazed over at the idea of being mayor for so long.

A moment later we pulled up to a large, white house. The sign said it was open for tours on Sunday afternoons. I made a note that we should definitely return on a Sunday and take the tour. I looked in my notebook and pulled out a paper I had printed from the Daughters of The Revolution. They took care of the mansion and I started reading about the house's history.

"This house was built by a wealthy Englishman for his bride Elizabeth Morris, and it was known as the White House Farm. His son, Anthony Walton White, went against family tradition and sided with the revolutionaries, against the British. The house was occupied during the revolution by the British, and still shows saber and musket marks on its floors, and banisters. After the revolution, it was owned by Col. Charles Stewart in the 1780s and was visited by several prominent men, such as George Washington, Alexander Hamilton, General Kosciusko, General Gates, and John Hancock. It was bought in 1821 by Col. Joseph Warren Scott, and it was home to his extended family for the next 90 years. He renamed the estate Buccleuch in honor of his Scottish lineage. The home and its grounds were left by his grandson to the city of New Brunswick for use as a public park, and to honor his grandfather. It opened as a museum in 1915, with its interior and furnishings maintained by Jersey Blue Daughters of the American Revolution, to promote the appreciation of American history."

"Stop the van," T-Bone shrieked when I told him there was a tunnel to the canal and it was on the US National Register of Historic Places. He pushed through the van until he reached the door and ran outside. Half of the van assumed he had to go to the bathroom and the rest thought he was car sick. I knew better. I knew the reason T-Bone had run out was because he heard people like George Washington and John Hancock had visited the house. He stood by the door, very quietly.

"Is he okay?" asked Michael.

"Yeah, he's fine," I laughed. "He's just imagining that he's speaking to George Washington."

"He really is a history buff, isn't he?" laughed Russell. "When he comes back, should we tell him the some of the dorms at Rutgers are named after signers of the Declaration of Independence?"

"Not unless you want to watch him have more moments at each dorm," my grandfather sighed.

"Hey, is anyone hungry?" asked Michael. "We have some amazing restaurants in this city, right Alexi?"

"We sure do," he agreed. "But I think we should take them to a very unique place."

"I bet I know what you're thinking about," Michael winked, as T-Bone rejoined the group.

They were definitely on the same page, because Alexi had a great big smile when we pulled over. They told us these were the famous Grease Trucks. I thought they were kidding, but they weren't. I wasn't sure if I wanted to eat from a grease truck, until I smelled the food and saw all of the people eating and smiling. Not only were the sandwiches amazing, they were a part of the Rutgers University culture. As soon as I grabbed my sandwich, I sat down to wait for everyone. A college student wearing sunglasses and carrying a backpack asked if he could sit on the opposite side of the table.

"What's up?" he said with a smile as he fished for something in his bag. "Nice day, huh?"

"Yeah," I said, a little nervous to talk to a college kid.

"Is this your first time visiting our grease trucks?" he asked.

"Yeah," I said, realizing I'd have to pick my end of the conversation up a bit. "We don't go to school here."

"I kind of figured that," he laughed. "My name is Joe Slezak."

"I'm Nicky," I answered. "Are you going to school in the summer?"

"Taking a couple of classes to get ahead," he explained. "But I miss my old summers when I was your age."

"Do you have to go to school in the summer?" I wondered.

"No, but sometimes it's hard to get the classes you need or you just want to get ahead," he said.

"What's your thing?" I asked, totally forgetting the word I was looking for.

"My major?" he smiled. "I'm studying meteorology, you know, weather and climate."

"You really wanna be a weatherman?" I asked, wondering if I'd see him on the news one day and then remember I had met him at the grease trucks.

"Not on camera," he laughed. "I'd rather be the guy handing the reports and information to the guy on camera. Plus, I like chasing storms."

"That's pretty cool," I nodded as he got in line.

He said goodbye and disappeared. I thought it was kind of funny how he just started talking to me. He must have been like T-Bone. I always thought college would be scary, but if everyone was as nice as he was, I figured it would be fine.

Suddenly, a man and a lady were standing next to me. When I started to make a big mess, the lady handed me a handful of napkins.

"Here, you'll need these," she smiled. "You can tell how good a sandwich is by the number of napkins you need."

"Thanks," I said, as I wiped my hands. "I'm Nicky."

I couldn't believe I had introduced myself to two total strangers. It was such a T-Bone thing to do.

"Hi, Nicky, I'm Sarah Neiderman and this is my husband, Rob," she smiled.

"Nice to meet you," he said in between bites.

"Do you guys eat here a lot?" I asked, shocked that I was holding up my end of the conversation with strangers.

"Well," she laughed, "we try to eat healthy, but every once in a while we find ourselves at this table."

"Oh, I'm sorry," I said. "Is this your table?"

"No, not at all," Rob replied. "We're happy to share."

By the time everyone returned from the different trucks, I had already made three new friends, all by myself. I decided to continue being assertive and asked Alexi some questions. In just a few minutes I learned that his favorite ice cream was orange blossom swirl, he loved to visit Seaside Heights and Jenkinson's Beach in Point Pleasant, he thought marble cake was good because it was the best of both worlds, and he thought New Brunswick was amazing. T-Bone was right, it was pretty easy to get to know people if you listen and let them tell you about themselves. This worked great for me since it meant less talking.

As soon as we left, Michael announced we would be driving by some very important New Brunswick history. He asked us if we were familiar with Johnson & Johnson. Having two younger sisters and a younger brother, I was definitely familiar with them. My mom always used their no more tears shampoo that didn't sting kids' eyes. Then I remembered T-Bone used the same shampoo.

"Kids this is Johnson Hall, the original Johnson & Johnson building. New Brunswick is the home of their Worldwide Headquarters and they have been a crucial part of our city and its success.

"Why? Do a lot of people here get shampoo in their eyes?" asked T-Bone.

"Actually, Johnson & Johnson creates many products and many jobs and when people are working they have more money to spend," Russell explained. "And when people have money to spend, a city needs more businesses and then that create more jobs. New Brunswick considers it an honor that this amazing company and the state university call our city home."

"How does somebody create such a big company?" I asked, in case I decided to start my own giant company. We had learned about so many amazing family businesses, from the Roeblings to the Kusers to the Valastros, that I thought I might like one, too, someday.

"Companies don't start out this big," Russell laughed. "It takes many years, good ideas, hard work, and dedication. Have you heard about a gentleman named General Robert Wood Johnson?"

"No," I admitted, not sure if I should've known him.

"I'll tell you a bit about him," he began, "and then I want you to visit a really interesting blog called www.KilmerHouse.com. Margaret Gurowitz is the Johnson & Johnson historian and she has put together a very complete set of information. She taught most of us everything we know about the Johnson Family."

"We'll definitely check that blog out," I said as I wrote the address in my notebook.

"So, in 1866, Johnson & Johnson was founded by the Johnson brothers, Robert Wood, James Wood, and Edward Mead, right here in New Brunswick. By 1888, they had published a book about keeping things sterile in surgery and changed the way people treated wounds in the US and around the world. This was also the year they invented the first commercial first aid kits. By 1894, they had launched maternity kits and baby powder."

"No way," T-Bone shrieked, "they invented baby powder? I love baby powder. I mean, I used to love baby powder, when I was a kid, I mean a baby."

"Not only that," he added. "They invented sterile uniforms, sterile surgical sutures, and they were the first to put toothpaste in a tube. They were the first to mass produce dental floss and first aid manuals, but 1921's invention is probably the product you know best. This is the year Band-Aids became available."

"I love Band-Aids," T-Bone exclaimed. "I mean I used to love them when I was a kid. Oh, forget it. Who am I kidding? I still love Band-Aids."

"It's okay," he smiled, "everyone loves them. "There were three brothers. When Robert Wood Johnson died rather suddenly, his brother James took over from 1910-1932. In 1932, General Robert Wood Johnson II, Robert Wood Johnson's son, took over."

"Wow, it must have been nice to have your dad give you a sweet position as the boss," I said, wishing my dad had a big company to give me.

"That isn't exactly how it went," Russell explained. "You see, General Robert Wood Johnson spent a lot of time at the company growing up. When he was sixteen years old, his dad died suddenly and he began working at the lowest job in the company, as a millhand, during the summer. He eventually worked his way up the ranks. His father had been a good role model; he walked home every day for lunch with the family, believed in the dignity of employees and rights of workers. He felt strongly that his company had a responsibility to patients, employees, consumers, and the community."

"That's pretty cool," said T-Bone. "He was rich and treated people nice? I bet all bosses aren't like that."

"Sadly, you're right," he agreed. "Many companies are only focused on profits. General Johnson followed his father's example and felt so strongly about a company's responsibility that he wrote something called Our Credo which still serves as the company's guiding philosophy. And, at a time when workers had little rights, he publicly called for higher minimum wages."

"His dad must have made a huge impression on him," I observed.

"His father told his children they were very, very privileged and because of that, they all had a responsibility to give back."

"There's also another person you should know about and that's Fred Kilmer, a scientist and the company's first Director of Scientific Affairs,"

Russell smiled. "He did more to advance health-care than anyone I can think of and he also had a very famous son."

"Was he related to Joyce Kilmer, the poet who wrote the famous poem, Trees?" I asked, shocking even myself that I remembered all of that from my grandmother.

"Actually, Alfred Joyce Kilmer was his son and yes, a very talented writer," he began. "The family lived here in New Brunswick and if you make an appointment, you can tour their home."

"Fred Kilmer gave so much to the world, but also to New Brunswick," Russ explained. "And he even had some pretty impressive friends, including Thomas Alva Edison."

"Seriously?" I looked at T-Bone. "I can't believe we just made another Thomas Edison connection.

"Absolutely," he nodded. "So much talent in one state; they could have lived anywhere and they chose New Jersey."

Fred Kilmer and General Robert Wood Johnson made so many contributions to our country and the world and he was right, they did it all in New

Jersey. One of the most impressive things we learned was about the Robert Wood Johnson Foundation. The General was apparently a very generous person and right before Christmas, in 1936, he took 12,000 shares of his company and formed the Johnson New Brunswick Foundation. Later, this organization became the Robert Wood Johnson Foundation and with $1.2 billion it was the largest philanthropy devoted to improving healthcare in America. I decided that very minute, if I ever had my own business, I would borrow his Credo and do the things he did.

While I couldn't believe how much of an impact Robert Wood Johnson had on our country, I also couldn't believe how amazing this bustling college town, often called Hub City, was. I asked about the theaters Alexi had mentioned in his letter and Russell drove us over to see them. The most famous were the State Theater and the George Street Playhouse, but there were many other good ones, too. Michael told us New Brunswick's theaters and shows were first class. He also explained how the arts were a very important part of New Brunswick's culture.

"You know, we have one of the finest art museums in the country," said Russell. "The Zimmerli Museum is renowned and we also have the Mason

Gross School of the Arts."

I was writing a note to myself to ask my parents to take us to a show, when I noticed the Helrich Hotel. It was a huge building in the middle of Monument Square which had a monument to the soldiers and sailors who served in the Civil War. It looked like a great place to stay. Michael told us about the many hospitals in New Brunswick, including Robert Wood Johnson and the Bristol Myers Squibb Children's Hospital.

"Before we wrap up the tour, is there anything else you'd like to show them?" Michael asked Alexi.

Alexi instructed them to drive us past Joyce Kilmer's house. Then we went by some famous restaurants, like the Frog and the Peach which dated back to 1876 and the Old Bay restaurant that was built in 1857 and housed the Bank of New Jersey until 1910. Alexi was excited to show us the public library that was built with a $50,000 gift from Andrew Carnegie in 1903. It has stained glass skylights and original metal shelving. The next stop was the train station, also constructed in 1903, and the last remaining Pennsylvania Railroad station for a mid-sized city in New Jersey.

Our last stop was Rutgers University's High Point Solutions Stadium. Michael told us about Eric LeGrand, the Rutgers player who was paralyzed from the neck down during a 2010 football game. T-Bone remembered reading that he was honored at the 2012 NJ Hall of Fame Induction and that he was signed by the Tampa Bay Buccaneers. Even though he couldn't play, he was an amazing example of strength, inspiration, and character for everyone. This was one more reason we loved the Hall of Fame; it wasn't just people from the past, it was also people that were impacting our state right now.

"Is he still on the team?" I asked.

"No," my grandfather explained. "He was signed as the 90th man and he retired so someone else could have his spot. He's a class act with true character."

"Did he get millions of dollars?" asked T-Bone.

"He didn't get any money," said my grandfather, "but his #52 jersey is available on the Buccaneers website with the money going to research for spinal cord injuries. He plans to finish his degree and become a sports broadcaster."

"That's an amazing story," I said. "He sounds like the most determined person in the world."

When we returned to City Hall, Alexi's mom and dad were waiting with his little sister, Diayana. His sister ran up to him as soon as he stepped out of the van. His parents looked so proud that he was sharing their city with us. We promised to send him a copy of our report and he told us to call him if we came back. We thanked everyone for the tour and couldn't wait to get home and write about it.

"That was awesome," I said as I sank into the car. I was exhausted, but we had learned so much and met so many great people. I wondered if I would go to Rutgers one day. If I did, I wanted to live in a dorm named after an actual signer of the Declaration of Independence and walk around the same town where General Robert Wood Johnson and his family, as well as the Kilmers lived.

I assumed we were heading home, but I was wrong. Instead of going home, my grandfather pulled up to a place called Thomas Sweet.

"What's this?" I asked.

"It's Thomas Sweet," said my grandfather, "and you boys are about to have a blend-in."

I didn't know what that meant, but since we were at an ice cream parlor I knew it would be good. We found out the blend-in was born, in 1979, as a Thomas Sweet original. The popular method of mixing favorite toppings with favorite flavors of ice cream began with Thomas Sweet, in Princeton, New Jersey. It's the first, and best, in the country!

It was amazing, I had vanilla with three kinds of candy bars while T-Bone blended gummy worms, nuts, and brownies. It wasn't what I would have picked, ever, but he really enjoyed it. My grand father, a Thomas Sweet veteran, insisted there was no better way to enjoy a topping than evenly spreading it throughout the ice cream. He was right. It was so good, I started wondering why I had never thought about blending in my toppings.

"This is amazing," T-Bone said as he scraped the side of his bowl with his spoon. "In all of my years of eating ice cream, I can't believe I never blended my toppings. I just let them sit up on top of the ice cream. After the first few bites, my toppings are gone. Why didn't I think of this?"

"You know they use a machine, right?" I laughed.

"Well, yeah," he shrugged, "I guess there's that."

"I was thinking the same thing," I admitted. "It's cool, though, that one of the best things to happen to ice cream first happened in New Jersey."

"Exactly," said T-Bone. "Even in the very, very important dessert department, New Jersey is revolutionary. What's your opinion Mr. A?"

"I think you both talk too much," my grandfather smiled as he continued scraping his bowl.

As we headed back to the turnpike, my grandfather made one last stop. It was the Rutgers University Bookstore. He walked right to the hat section, grabbed three Rutgers baseball hats and proceeded to the register. When the clerk started to put the hats in a bag, he told her that wouldn't be necessary. We slipped our new hats on and headed home... *three new Rutgers fans.*

Chapter Six

NJ TRANSIT

"Nicky, Nicky," my sisters screamed. "Nicky, mom says you have to get up."

"What?" I asked. I was so tired I couldn't pry my eyes open.

"Mom says you have to wake up, now!"

I started rubbing my eyes and yawning at the same time. I couldn't understand why my mom was waking me up so early. It took me a minute to roll out of bed and when I could finally focus, I realized it was almost lunchtime.

"Well, good afternoon, sleepyhead," my mom

laughed as she carried a pile of clothes into my room. "Were you planning on waking up today?"

"I can't believe I slept so long," I said in between a chain of yawns. "Is that clock really right?"

"It sure is," she smiled. "You must have had an amazing adventure in New Brunswick yesterday."

"Mom, it was really cool. They have historic houses, the Delaware & Raritan Canal runs along the Raritan River, there's the arts, the train station, Johnson & Johnson, General Robert Wood Johnson, Alfred Joyce Kilmer and Rutgers all in one city."

"That's great, dear," she said. "I'm glad you had a good time. So what's on your agenda for what's left of the day?"

"T-Bone's coming over later so we can get some more ideas for day trips and for his campaign."

"Honey, T-Bone's been downstairs for two hours," she said as she walked out.

I went downstairs and there he was, sitting at the kitchen table playing rummy with my brother, Timmy.

"Good morning, sunshine," he joked. "I came over early because I have a good idea."

"You come over early every day," I said through another yawn.

"But this time I have a reason," he explained. "I was thinking about places to visit and this is going to blow your mind."

"Okay," I sighed. "Where's this place?"

"Places," he corrected.

"How many?" I asked, fighting off another yawn.

"A lot," he answered.

"What's a lot?"

"Almost every county," he smirked.

"You can't seriously want to visit twenty-one counties in one trip, can you?"

"Not exactly," he shook his head. "But they do have these things in almost every county."

"Wawa?" I asked, referring to my most favorite

convenience store and humming the Hoagie-fest song.

"Not exactly," he continued. "I'm talking about New Jersey Transit."

"You want to visit trains and buses?" I asked.

"Not exactly" he explained. "I'm talking about train stations."

"But how do we do a day trip about train stations?" I asked.

"I don't know. Let's ride every single train and check out the stations," he suggested. "How many stations could there possibly be?"

We headed to the computer and started searching for information.

"Wow," I said as I read from NJ TRANSIT's web page. "Covering a service area of 5,325 square miles, NJ TRANSIT is the nation's third largest provider of bus, rail and light rail transit, linking major points in New Jersey, New York and Philadelphia."

"I don't know," T-Bone shook his head. "That might be a lot of trains."

"It might be?" I laughed and continued reading. "The agency operates a fleet of 2,027 buses, 711 trains and 45 light rail vehicles. With 236 bus routes and 11 rail lines statewide, NJ TRANSIT provides nearly 223 million passenger trips each year."

"Wow, that's unbelievable," he shrieked. "They have thousands of buses and hundreds of trains! That would probably take longer than a day."

"You know, trains have been around a long time," I said, "so maybe we should start with their history and why they're so important to the state."

I knew when I said the word history, T-Bone would smile. He did. We read about a familiar man, Colonel John Stevens. We learned about him during our trip to Hoboken to visit Tessy Colegrove and her famous family. In 1826, Stevens proved steam locomotion would work on a circular experimental track constructed on his estate in Hoboken. In 1815, he was granted the first railroad charter in North America. Grants to others followed, and work soon began on the first operational railroads.

"Is this the same John Stevens that bought the "island" of Hoboken in 1783 and then transformed it into a waterfront resort? The same Stevens the famous Stevens Institute is named after? The same Stevens who owned a mansion on the bluff that is no longer there?" asked T-Bone.

I was speechless. How did he remember all these details? We didn't realize he was the Father of the American Railroad. I was pretty excited to know that New Jersey also gave the country railroads.

"Yes," I answered all three of his questions with one word. "How cool is that?"

"Cool enough to take me up on my idea?" he smiled.

"More than cool enough," I said, excited to learn about our important role in history. "Let's keep searching."

We knew from our adventures that there were a lot of train stations all over the state. Some were huge like Newark Penn Station and Secaucus Junction and some were really tiny and in the center of towns. I could never decide what kind of train stations I liked best; the busy Grand-Central-style stations or the small, looks-like-they-were-plucked-from-a-snow-globe kind. As small as New Jersey was, NJ TRANSIT ran 161 stations. I was floored. There were only twenty-one counties and that seemed like a huge number for actual stations. Just the very famous, 58.1 mile long, Northeast Corridor line had seventeen stations between Trenton and New York.

I wondered if kids and families actually thought about using trains instead of driving. It seemed so logical; it was less expensive than driving, saved wear and tear on cars, allowed people to better use the time they would spend driving, reduced pollution, and let's face it, it was fun.

We decided from now on, we would see if we could take trains or buses on some of our day trips. Besides all of the amazing reasons, for taking trains, I knew this would allow us to see some of the train stations.

"You know," T-Bone began, "without trains, our country wouldn't have grown nearly as fast as it did."

"I know," I agreed. "And they're still important. Millions of people use trains to get to work or as their main way of getting around. Especially in cities where many people don't own cars. Plus, it's definitely much better for the environment."

"Hey, that's not good," T-Bone gasped.

"No, it is," I said. "When people use trains instead of cars, we don't use as much gasoline and we don't cause as much pollution. Everyone knows that."

"No, no," he said with a new sense of urgency, "I just came across an article about kids trespassing on train tracks and getting seriously hurt."

"Why would they be on train tracks?" I asked.

"Well, it says here that some kids walk on tracks or aren't careful when crossing tracks," he explained.

I couldn't believe it. Trains were awesome and so important and there was really no reason for anyone to be hit by a train. T Bone read that many kids think they can outrun a moving train. They didn't realize trains travel much faster than they appeared and create an optical illusion to be moving slow. We also read about kids who try to surf on top of trains. Holy stupidity, I thought. These trains were electrified with high voltage catenary wires. There were signs everywhere and kids should have enough common sense to stay away from trains and off tracks. At least that's what I thought.

As we kept searching, we came across something interesting that immediately caught our attention. NJ TRANSIT was so concerned about people, especially kids, trespassing on tracks that they developed their own Safety Education Program. It said they visit hundreds of New Jersey public, private, and charter schools each year and they conduct complimentary presentations including first-person stories. High school kids would now hear from a NJ TRANSIT engineer and a police officer who witnessed a rail fatality. It sounded heavy, but there was just no way to sugar-coat something so dangerous. I started thinking.

"Maybe we could help," I suggested. "I think we should call NJ TRANSIT and speak to the person in charge of keeping kids safe. We should ask a lot of questions and then do a report for the website."

"Good idea," said T-Bone. "Can I make that part of my platform?"

"You wanna run for student council on the issue of kids staying away from tracks and crossing carefully?" I asked.

"Sure," he nodded. "Why, no good?"

"Well, I doubt any of the other candidates would

disagree with you, but we don't really have tracks near our school," I said.

"Okay," he countered, "first, kids go all over the state and we've seen so many places that have tracks going right through the town. Second, kids can tell their friends and relatives about this. And third, can I only stand for things that happen at our school and in our town?"

He raised two very good points and I didn't have an answer to the last question. Having never been a campaign manager, I had no idea what issues he should talk about. Even though it wasn't the typical less homework, better food in the cafeteria issue, it was definitely important.

"You know what?" I agreed, "You've convinced me. It's really important and none of your opponents will be ready for it. You should do it."

We called NJ TRANSIT and T-Bone asked for the person in charge of keeping kids safe. A cheerful receptionist connected us to Miss Grace and Miss Barbara. They visit schools, educating kids about the danger of being near or on tracks. They were very passionate about their job and work very hard at spreading safety messages throughout the state. They explained the dangers weren't limited to kids taking shortcuts across tracks, but also that kids sometimes crossed when the gates are down. We learned that when gates are down and a train passed by, many people, including kids, went under the gates, too impatient to wait for the gates to go up again. They didn't realize a second train was coming from the opposite direction.

"You mean they waited for the first train to pass and got hit by a second train?" T-Bone gasped.

"Unfortunately, yes," she said. "A *second train coming* is a very real danger and the reason gates remain down. Sadly, some motorists make that mistake, too, and there's not enough time to get out of the way."

We were shocked. Because I didn't live near train tracks and cross them frequently, I assumed everyone was super careful. But I figured it was like everything else in life; once you got used to something, you took it for granted. Apparently, people took the danger for granted, too.

"Miss Grace," T-Bone began, "hypothetically, if you and Miss Barbara were running for student council and wanted to make train safety part of your platform, what would you tell kids?"

"Are you, by any chance, hypothetically running for student council?" she laughed.

"Actually, yes," he said, "and even though many candidates limit their positions to school issues, I want to make sure everyone in my school knows the dangers about trains and tracks. Once they know, they can tell other kids. Plus, Nicky and I are the soon-to-be Official Junior Ambassadors of New Jersey and we have lots of fans we can tell."

"Well, I didn't know I was speaking with two New Jersey celebrities," she said.

"We're not celebrities," I interrupted. "We just find great New Jersey places, visit them, and write about them on. The state puts them on a website and people follow our adventures."

"What a wonderful service you're doing for the state," she said. "Have you ever thought about including train, light rail, and bus service as part of your reports? Miss Barbara and I would be happy to help you."

"We've taken trains and the light rail before," I informed her. "But we didn't realize NJ TRANSIT could bring people to so many places across the state. We'll definitely do a report."

"Before you write your report, did you know we also have beach and other packages and we offer specials where kids ride free?"

"Did not know that," said T-Bone as he frantically took notes.

"Check out www.njtransit.com and you'll see the specials available all year long at our Deals and Destinations," she suggested.

"Will do," we said as we prepared to hang up.

"And, by the way," she said, "hypothetically, if I attended your school, you would hypothetically get my real vote."

I had to hand it to T-Bone, not only did he have a really interesting idea, it was also an important idea. Sharing amazing places with kids and their families felt great, but keeping kids safe was even better.

"What are you doing?" I asked as T-Bone sat in front of the computer.

"Take a guess," he smiled.

"Figuring out a way to allow Miss Grace and Miss

118

Barbara to vote in the student council election?" I guessed.

"Even better," he said. "I'm doing something your dad would definitely appreciate."

I wasn't sure what that meant until I peeked at the screen to see what he was looking at... *Deals and Destinations.*

Chapter Seven

Princeton & Kingston

After several hours of transit research, we decided to stop and beg my mom to order a pizza. I even had a coupon for free delivery and five dollars off of our order. I was too late. She was putting on the oven mitts and opening the oven door. I wasn't sure what was in there, but the smell was finally hitting my nose.

"What is that?" asked T-Bone as he held his nose.

"The key to living longer," my mom smiled and gently set a casserole dish on the counter.

"No, really," T-Bone insisted, "is that the self-cleaning oven smell?"

"No, I tried a new recipe," she smiled, as Timmy and Emma came in holding their noses.

"Mom, that stinks," I agreed. "That's what you want us to eat for dinner?"

"Well, it has so many super-foods and healthy ingredients," she said as she waved the smoke away, sending the stink right to our noses. "I think we should give it a try."

"What's that horrow-ful smell?" asked Maggie as she entered the kitchen. "Is the garbage truck in my house?"

"No, dear," my mom sighed, realizing she couldn't talk us out of un-smelling it.

Just then my dad walked in with two giant pizzas. The bad smell from that casserole was stronger than the good smell from the pizzas.

"What's that smell?" my dad asked as he squinted. "I think it's burning my eyes."

"Mom made something healthy," I laughed.

"She used super glue," said Emma.

"No, dear," my mom smiled as she blew the hair out of her eyes, "I tried to make a casserole with super foods."

"I think you made one with super smelly foods," my dad laughed. "Seriously, what is that?"

Before she could answer, something caught her eye. It was T-Bone, holding a small plate filled with the mystery dish.

"You know," he nodded and swallowed, "it's not that bad. If you replaced the vegetables with some ground beef and ricotta cheese, and replaced this white stuff with actual mozzarella cheese, and maybe put a tomato sauce over it, you might have something here."

"Yeah, you'd have a lasagna," my dad laughed. "Why don't we put that casserole outside and have some pizza."

It was like my dad was reading my mind and not a minute too soon. Ten minutes later and she would have been spooning her slop onto our plates. As soon as the odor left the kitchen, my dad started passing out slices.

"Nick," said my dad, "your grandfather called me

today and wanted to see if you boys were available tomorrow."

"Why? What's up?" I asked.

"He has a day trip he's been working on and he wants to surprise you," he replied.

"Where to?" T-Bone wondered out loud.

"Wouldn't be much of a surprise if I told you, would it?" my dad winked and changed the subject.

I was kind of excited to see what he planned for us, although it would be weird not knowing what we were doing. The next morning, T-Bone arrived, thankfully, not wearing a suit. His hair was slicked to the side and his teeth were still bordering on radioactive, but at least he wasn't wearing his suit.

"Since I wasn't sure where we were going, I didn't know what to wear," said T-Bone. "I brought a bathing suit, flip flops, a towel and a sweatshirt."

"Great," said my grandfather, "you won't need any of them."

"So, no beach, no pool, and no water park?" asked T-Bone. "Hmmm."

"No, sir," my grandfather smiled and kept walking toward the car.

We headed north on 295 and took the Princeton Pike exit. My grandfather pointed out amazing spots. The road cut right through the Princeton Battlefield and my grandfather pulled over.

"You boys have had plenty of practice playing tour guide" said my grandfather as he pulled out a stack of index cards. "Now, it's my turn and by the way, you can even find this information on the Department of Environmental Protection's website. On January 3, 1777, the peaceful winter fields and woods of Princeton Battlefield were transformed into the site of what is considered to be the fiercest fight of its size during the American Revolution. During this most desperate battle, American troops under Gen. George Washington surprised and defeated a force of British Regulars. Coming at the end of "The Ten Crucial Days" which saw the well-known night crossing of the Delaware River and two battles in Trenton, the Battle of Princeton gave Washington his first victory against the British Regulars on the field. The battle extended over a mile away to the College of New Jersey which is now Princeton University."

"But I thought we had already beat the British in the two Battles of Trenton," said T-Bone.

"No, we beat the Hessians," said my grandfather. "They were the well-trained, professional soldiers from Germany that Great Britain paid to fight the war. The Battle of Princeton was where we beat the British Regulars."

"If the Hessians were so well-trained and we were, what's the word I'm kinda looking for, *not-so-well-trained,* then how did we win?" I wondered.

"Well, there's a lot to be said about defending your own land as opposed to fighting someone else's war where you have nothing personal at stake," my grandfather began.

"Then of course, there was the brilliant surprise of it all. And, let's not forget that the Hessians weren't all in one spot. Those soldiers were spread throughout the city in citizen's homes. By the time they realized what was happening, it was too late."

"Does it say all of that on that card in your hand?" I asked, noticing there were only a couple of words on the card.

"No," he smiled, "I saw that on a PBS special.

These are keywords. Whenever I had to speak in public, I always wrote down keywords instead of a speech. I found it too hard to keep track of my place and look up. This way, I see a word and know what I want to talk about and I can actually look at my audience and talk to them instead of talking at them."

"Hey, can I use that trick for my debates?" T-Bone asked.

"I think that's a wonderful idea," my grandfather agreed. "Now, as we continue down this road, we'll come across an important home. It's still a private residence, but 112 Mercer Street was the home of Albert Einstein."

"No way," I said. "Albert Einstein lived here?"

"He taught at the university and he even lived here," my grandfather explained. "He had accepted an invitation from educator Abraham Flexner to study in America. Flexner's idea was to create a place where physicists and mathematicians could ponder the nature of the world while remaining free from the world's cares and free from having to teach. He called this haven the Institute for Advanced Study, endowed it and set it up on the Princeton University campus. Einstein is famous for many things, among them, of course, the theory of relativity. If you've ever seen $E = mc^2$, that's his equation. He also won the Nobel Prize in 1921. Ironically, it's been said that he was also absent-minded and often forgot things."

"How could someone so smart forget things?" I wondered. "And are you telling me he got paid to think?"

"Well, they say he was so intelligent, he often forgot everyday things. There's a story that a man once called the Dean's Office, looking for directions to Einstein's house. When the man on the other end of the phone explained he could not give that information out, the man told him *he was Albert Einstein* and he had gotten lost walking home."

"And they paid him to think?" I repeated.

"And they got their money's worth," my grandfather laughed. "He's probably one of the smartest people that ever lived."

"So you're saying science was as important to him as history is to me," T-Bone inquired.

"You would think that," my grandfather smiled, rummaging through his cards. "But actually, I have a couple of his quotes that may give you more insight into Einstein the man. He said if I were not a physicist, I would probably be a musician. I often think in music. I live my daydreams in music. I see my life in terms of music.... I do know that I get most joy in life out of my violin."

"Really? Music?" I asked in disbelief.

"Music is an amazing tool," my grandfather explained. "Then again, imagination is also. Einstein once said I am enough of an artist to draw freely upon my imagination. Imagination is more important than knowledge. Knowledge is limited. Imagination encircles the world."

"Very cool," T-Bone and I agreed, never having put much thought into the importance of imagination.

My grandfather made a left on Library Place and a left on the Stockton Street which was also Route 206. We pulled up in front of a very stately home. I couldn't believe it. We were finally in front of Drumthwacket, the Official Residence of the Governor. I remembered when T-Bone thought we would be hired to rake the leaves and, after seeing the size of the place, was happy they never asked. The land was once owned by William Penn, a Quaker that I was very familiar with; he founded my old colony of Pennsylvania. My grandfather had many details prepared and ready to be shared.

He told us that Charles Smith Olden, a very wealthy businessman, started construction of Drumthwacket in 1835. The name was Scottish for wooded hill. It was originally a center hall with two rooms on each side. Mr. Olden was very involved in the community and even served as treasurer and Trustee of the College of New Jersey, now known as Princeton University. He served as State Senator and was elected New Jersey's 19th Governor in 1860. He was the very first governor to live at Drumthwacket.

In 1893, a banker and industrialist named Moses Taylor Pyne bought the home from Mr. Olden's widow for about $15,000. He immediately started transforming it into the estate it would become and the biggest in Princeton at the time. He added a library, hundreds of acres, park-like landscaping, greenhouses, a dairy farm, and formal Italian gardens.

"Wow, that cost less than a new car," said T-Bone. "He got a pretty good deal."

"Of course, $15,000 in 1893 was a lot of money," my grandfather laughed.

Once he explained the difference in value, my grandfather continued the estate's history. In 1941, Abraham Nathaniel Spanel bought the house and surrounding 12 acres from Mr. Pyne's only grandchild, Agnes. He was a scientist that founded the International Latex Corporation and his rubber products were critical to the success of the World War II effort. Many of his inventions were created in what is, today, the music room.

Finally, in 1966, the Spanel family sold the Drumthwacket estate to the State of New Jersey with the intent that it be used as the Official Residence of the Governor. It took until 1981 to raise the funds and in 1982 the Drumthwacket Foundation was formed. They are responsible for preserving and maintaining the home and grounds which are listed on the National Register of Historic Places.

"Hold on," I said. "Governor Olden was the first Governor to live there. Then families lived there after him. So, where did the governors live before it was finished?"

"I'll show you," my grandfather winked and turned around to head down Stockton Street toward Nassau Street.

We arrived in front of the Morven Museum and Garden, another beautiful white house. My grandfather skimmed his cards and told us that this home had played a role in our state's history for over 200 years. It was part of 5,500 acres that were also owned by William Penn and the tract was purchased in 1701 by the first Richard Stockton. In 1754, his grandson, also Richard Stockton, an attorney and one of New Jersey's five signers of the Declaration of Independence, acquired 150 acres of the land for a house.

Four more generations of Stocktons lived in the house through the early twentieth century. While all of the Stocktons contributed to the community, the most famous was Commodore Robert Stockton who was a United States Naval hero and President of the Delaware & Raritan Canal.

"There was a president of the canal?" asked T-Bone. "Do the Stocktons still live here?"

"No," my grandfather explained. "The next person to reside here is someone that may be of interest to you, it was General Robert Wood Johnson."

"No way," we said together.

"It's true," my grandfather smiled. "In fact, he was

the first non-family member to reside here from 1928 through 1944. He was followed by five other New Jersey Governors from 1945-1981. The last governor to live there was Gov. Brendan Byrne. Morven is also a designated National Historic Landmark."

"So if I become Governor one day," said T-Bone, "I'll move to Drumthwacket?"

"If you want," said my grandfather. "It's not mandatory. Some governors choose to stay in their own homes and use the estate to entertain or for formal dinners and occasions."

"No way," said T-Bone, "if, I mean, when I become Governor, I'm moving right in. If I'm the Governor, can I order my brothers to become my butlers?"

"I'd have to take a look at the state constitution," my grandfather laughed.

"The state what?" I asked. "Don't you mean the United States Constitution?"

"No, New Jersey has its own constitution," he said. "Those are the laws of the state in addition to the United States Constitution which are the laws that govern the country."

"I hope the constitution makes it a law that my brothers have to do everything I say," T-Bone daydreamed out loud. "If not, I'll just make an executive order."

We continued to Nassau Street and my grandfather parked the car. We walked around the historic campus of Princeton University, the oldest university in the state and fourth oldest in the country. Established in 1746, it has been the home of many notable alumni, including Supreme Court justices, business leaders, governors, and even famous actors.

The campus was made up of really old buildings with open grassy areas and it was surrounded by a pretty lively town. We headed to the Yankee Doodle Tap Room at the Nassau Inn, a hotel in the center of Palmer Square. My grandfather seemed like he knew exactly where he was going and he did. We entered the restaurant and he pointed to a wall filled with pictures. They were pictures of the famous university alumni that stayed at the hotel. It was an impressive list and even included some very famous people. I knew T-Bone was imagining his picture up on that wall. Of course, that would be after he was inducted to the New Jersey Hall of Fame and elected Governor.

We stayed for lunch and noticed names were carved into the wood tables. Our waitress told us many famous alumni carved their names in the table. T-Bone thought it was a crime, but she explained it was a tradition. The food was great and it had that colonial tavern feel that we really liked. While T-Bone imagined his face on the wall, I imagined having a conversation with George Washington and, even Benjamin Franklin; which according to Albert Einstein was a very important thing to do.

When we returned to Palmer Square, we walked past the shops and restaurants and T-Bone stopped in his tracks.

"What is it?" I asked.

"There it is," he said. "There it is."

"What is it?" I repeated.

"Thomas Sweet," he exclaimed. "Just like in New Brunswick. There it is!"

He was right and we headed straight there. I decided to order the same exact thing I had ordered at Thomas Sweet in New Brunswick. T-Bone went more exotic this time, blending bananas, coconut, and pecans. While we waited to order, I recognized a man from the other store.

T-Bone, wasted no time introducing us and we learned the man was Marco Cucchi, the owner. He smiled when T-Bone told him about our ambassadorship and he gave us a coupon for a free blend-in next time we were in town. We thanked him and suggested that, if he was still looking for more locations, our school might be a good idea.

"I've got to hand it to you, Pop, this was a pretty great tour of Princeton," I said. "You know, a kid named Blake Hanrahan from Mount Laurel suggested we come here. Between New Brunswick and Princeton, I'm realizing how much I like historic college towns."

"What are you thanking me for now?" he asked. "The tour's not over. Our next stop is north, up Route 27 to the nearby town of Kingston."

"Was that short for King's Town?" asked T-Bone. "And would that make Princeton short for Prince's Town?"

"Sure," he nodded, not even paying attention to the question. "So we're going to a place called Historic Rockingham."

"I like it already," T-Bone laughed.

"As we're driving over there, I'll give you a little of the history," he said. "Rockingham was General George Washington's last war-time headquarters from August through November 1783. It was at this site that he wrote the very famous "Farewell Orders to the Armies of the United States" which formally ended the Revolutionary War."

"So he definitely stayed there?" I tried to confirm. My grandfather nodded.

We pulled up to a large farmhouse and garden, right along the Delaware & Raritan Canal. We waited for our tour guide and he invited us inside. The house was as I had pictured it to be and I wondered if the family who actually owned it stayed there when the general and his aides moved in, like the Ford Family at the Ford Mansion in Morristown. He explained that it was originally built by New Jersey Supreme Court Justice, John Berrien and when he died, he left the property to his wife, Margaret. In 1783, she had put the property up for sale, but agreed to rent it to General Washington on a monthly basis.

"You know what's so great about this house?" T-Bone asked the tour guide.

Before the gentleman could even speak, T-Bone answered his own question.

"We're history buffs and we've been to a lot of historic houses and this house is really amazing," he began.

"But what's really great is that General George Washington stayed right here. And I'm sure he had famous visitors, too."

"He sure did," the guide explained. "Washington entertained frequently including Congressmen such as James Madison and Elias Boudinot, military personnel such as Generals Nathaniel Greene and Benjamin Lincoln, Revolutionaries Robert Morris and Thomas Paine, and local acquaintances such as Annis Stockton, widow of Declaration of Independence signer, Richard Stockton, and the Van Hornes. He even hosted at least one party with nearly two-hundred guests in early September. He, as well as Martha, also sat for two portraits at Rockingham."

"I wish I could have been at that party," I said, taking Albert Einstein's advice and imagining myself mingling with our Founding Fathers.

When we finished our tour of the house, we walked

through the kitchen garden. It reminded me of the kitchen garden at the William Trent House in Trenton. Afterward, we walked to the back of the property and came upon the Delaware & Raritan Canal, again.

"This canal is everywhere," I laughed. "For most of my life, I never even knew it existed. Now, ever since I've learned about it, I can't stop seeing it! I'm starting to feel like this canal is following me."

"I think you're seeing that so many aspects of New Jersey's past are connected to each other and, more importantly, connected to our future," my grandfather wisely noted. "One of New Jersey's greatest assets is its size. So much variety in a relatively small state."

There was something very special about Princeton. Much like the towns of New Brunswick, Trenton, Morristown, and Burlington, you could feel the history. And more than that, you could feel the importance. My grandfather was right, New Jersey's past and present were completely connected and these places proved it.

The remainder of our trip consisted of checking out Lake Carnegie, where the crew teams competed and the Visitors Center on Nassau Street in the historic Bainbridge house. They told us when we come back to check out the Clark House and take a guided walking tour. It definitely sounded like a good idea. We headed to University Place where he pointed out the famous McCarter Theater and the Princeton train station. We told my grandfather about our new interest in transportation and trains and he suggested we find the train station whenever we visited a town, if the town had one.

He told us the one-car DINKY train connected this little train station to the Princeton Junction stop on the Northeast Corridor line. It was a five minute ride that made it convenient for students and residents to commute from the center of town. Since many students didn't have vehicles, this was a necessity as well as a Princeton tradition.

Our last stop of the day was dinner. It was already after five o'clock and T-Bone was getting a little edgy. My grandfather knew what was happening and had a plan. We drove one mile from the DINKY to a very well-known place called Hoagie Haven. Apparently, everyone who lived in, worked in, or attended school in Princeton knew this was the place to get a great hoagie. They were right. The hoagie was big, fresh, and delicious, exactly the way I like it. We sat on a bench out front, people-watching and eating.

As I started eating, I imagined what it would be like if every famous person who spent time in Princeton showed up at the Hoagie Haven at the same time. I wondered what someone like General Washington or President Woodrow Wilson would have said to each other. I wondered what T-Bone would have said to Governor Stockton. I even wondered what Albert Einstein would have said to me. *Probably good work with imagining, now has anyone seen my violin?*

Chapter Eight

Government in Action

The next day, as we began preparing our Princeton report, my mom called us to the family room.

She had two envelopes in one hand and a note in the other. Being huge fans of fan mail, we asked for the envelopes first. The first was a dvd and post cards from four boys from Harrison Elementary School in Livingston. The letter said Mrs. Orozco was submitting a rap and postcards in support of the bill to name us Official Junior Ambassadors. We looked at each other, looked at my mom, and then raced to the computer. I slid the DVD in and we watched Jimmy Souffront, Michael Petrillo, Jake Cohen and Josh Minion rap about us. It was awesome. Mrs. Orozco wrote that this was a copy and that several copies were sent to the State House. These guys were pretty cool and T-Bone and I could not believe they went to all of that trouble to help us.

The next envelope was from three students from Mrs. Welsh's fourth grade at Delaware Township Elementary School in Sergeantsville. Lauren Bruhl, Marissa Matteo, and Hailey Becker wrote a rap and created an awesome poster with flip up post cards and pictures of places we have visited. They went to a lot of trouble and it came out great. As usual, my mom wanted to frame it, but T-Bone made an unusual request; he wanted to bring it home and hang it on his refrigerator. I agreed that he could take it, but I had one regret. I wished I had thought of it sooner.

"What about the note?" I asked my mom.

"Oh, Billy just called from the State House," she began.

"He said he has a surprise, but don't get too excited, they haven't voted for you yet. He said to go ahead and check out www.nickyfifth.com."

"What's that?" I asked.

"I guess we'll find out as soon as you type it," she smiled.

T-Bone and I were confused, but we followed Billy's directions. We couldn't believe it. We had our own website. I was shocked and impressed at the same time. I loved it. T-Bone, however, wanted to know where his name was.

"Billy said to call him after you log on," my mom instructed.

T-Bone looked upset and I felt bad that they only used my name on the site. Luckily, they had pictures of both of us on the front page. Billy was so excited to tell us about this latest development.

"Hey, guys," he said, "did you see the website yet?"

"We're looking at it now," I replied while T-Bone sat there, much quieter than usual.

"Okay, let me start from the beginning," he said. "While we're waiting for you to become Official Junior Ambassadors, we thought it would be exciting to give you your own website. We've learned about so many schools that are reading about your adventures and this will help you connect with your fans."

Even the word fans didn't make T-Bone smile. I knew this was serious.

"Excuse me, Billy," I interrupted. "Shouldn't the website be named Nicky Fifth and T-Bone?"

"That's definitely too long," he laughed. "I just wrote both of your names down on pieces of paper and randomly pulled out three of them. I decided to go with the best out of three."

I thought T-Bone would run out of my house when he heard the website was named randomly. Instead, he nodded his head and said, "Cool. That's fair." It turned out he wasn't upset that his name wasn't on the website, his feelings were hurt because he didn't know why. Now that he knew why and especially, that my name was picked fair and square, he was back to being excited.

"Now, there's more news," he said. "We've assigned a very talented web designer named Allyssa Barnes to help you make an amazing website. I have to approve everything, but start coming up with more ideas to impact kids and families and Allyssa will get it on the site."

"Really?" we asked, not able to fully grasp the incredible opportunity we had been given.

"Absolutely," he said. "If you have great ideas run them by me and then we'll talk to Allyssa."

"Is she our employee?" I asked.

"No," he laughed, "but she's super talented and excited to work with you."

"I have an idea," said T-Bone. "You may not know this, Billy, but I'm running for office."

"That's fantastic. I had no idea that in addition to New Jersey, you were also interested in politics," he said. "What office are you running for?"

"Well, I was planning to run for the New Jersey Hall of Fame," T-Bone explained. "But then Nick's dad told me that wasn't a real political office. Then I was thinking about General Assembly or Senate, and I realized I wasn't old enough. Then Mrs. A. said I should run for student council."

"That's fantastic," said Billy. "What made you decide to run for office?"

"I want to do things that help New Jersey and people in New Jersey," T-Bone answered.

"That's the best reason," Billy agreed. "If you need

any advice, just let me know."

"Thanks again for the website," I said as we hung up.

Billy told us to keep up the good work and we promised to come up with more ideas. Ten minutes later, T-Bone had one.

"You know how I want to be a politician?" he began. "And how I didn't even know the age requirement to be a Senator or a member of the General Assembly? Do you believe I didn't know that?"

"In your defense," I shrugged, "I doubt most people know the answers to those questions."

"That's my point," he insisted. "What do most people, who aren't history buffs and aren't excited about politics, actually know about it? Don't you think we should do something about politics and government on our website?"

"I don't know," I paused. "Don't they say never talk about religion or politics?"

"Who's they?" T-Bone quizzed me. "And if we don't talk about politics and religion, how will anyone know what's going on? Wasn't this country settled by people searching for religious freedom? Didn't they want everyone to respect people's choices? Don't you need to know about something to truly respect it? And wasn't this country founded by people who talked about politics? Didn't they meet at taverns to exchange their ideas? Aren't most wars started over religion or politics? If you ask me, not talking about it isn't the answer."

"Okay, okay, I guess it's not a bad idea," I agreed. "In fact, you're right about both of them. I think the trick is reminding people that they don't have to agree, but they have to listen respectfully and when it comes to politics, people should base their opinions on facts. But what would you want to include?"

"I guess we should start with Colonial days and the first governors," he began. "Then we can teach them about the Continental Congress and the Declaration of Independence and then..."

"Hold on," I interrupted. "You can't go back to the Mayflower to get people interested in today's politics. I think you should only talk about politics today."

"I disagree," said T-Bone. "In fact, let's conduct an experiment. Follow me."

We walked outside and sat on my front steps. I wasn't sure what he was planning, but I knew it would be a disaster. Soon, a girl I had never seen before came walking down my street. T-Bone noticed her and quickly asked me who she was. I looked once more and told him I had never seen her before. "Perfect," he said as he casually strolled toward her.

"Excuse me," he said as she approached. "Do you mind if I ask you a question?"

"That depends," she said, "do mind if I totally ignore you and pretend to think about an answer before I walk away saying nothing?"

"Actually, yes, I would mind," he said. "Plus, if you're going to think about it, why not tell me your answer?"

"Listen, genius," she said, standing ten inches from his nose, "first of all, I said I would pretend to think about it. I never said I would actually think about it. And second of all, who are you?"

"Okay," he said, rolling his eyes at me while he tried to regroup, "my name is T-Bone and this is my friend, Nicky. And if you're going to take the time to pretend to think, why not just think?"

"T-Bone? You're named after a steak?" she laughed. "What's the matter, filet mignon was already taken?"

"No," he made a face and shook his head, "my real name is Tommy Rizzo. Actually, they call me T-Bone because my name starts with *T*."

"Yeah, I get that. Very original," she said with a level of sarcasm that was much more powerful than what I usually doled out.

"You know you can't control the nickname people give you," said T-Bone, trying to defend himself.

"Listen, T-Bird," she said, "just ask me your question so I can forget this conversation ever happened."

"Okay, it's T-Bone," he explained, "and, I uh, um, I, I think I forgot the question."

"You're a real piece of work," she said. "But do me a favor, Pot Roast and friend, Nicky, next time you see me, close your eyes until I pass by."

"Ooh, I remember the question," he frantically jumped up. "And just for the record, it's *T-Bone*. So, what can you tell me about New Jersey's government, like the General Assembly and the Senate?"

"That's depends, "she confidently smirked. "Do you want to know about requirements for running, salary, current members, or party allegiance?"

T-Bone was dumbfounded and speechless. This was worse than when he met Buddy Valastro and Mama. He just stared straight ahead. I couldn't tell if he hated her or had just fallen in love.

"So, T-Rex, I guess you can ask questions, but you just can't answer them?" she observed.

"What was the question?" he asked.

"What do you want me to tell you about the General Assembly or the Senate?" she demanded.

"Whatever you want," he said, smiling and staring at her.

"Okay, I'll talk slower because it looks like you have a hard time keeping up," she began. "The state of New Jersey has three branches of government; the Executive, the Legislative, and the Judicial. Basically, that means we have a Governor, two houses of legislators, and a Supreme

Court. The two houses, or chambers, are the General Assembly and the Senate. Their job is to write laws. The court's job is to interpret the laws and make sure they're constitutional. A governor is supposed to lead. Any questions?"

"Just one," said T-Bone. "What's your name?"

"Wanda," she said as she walked away. "See you later, friend Nicky. Good-bye T-Shirt."

And just like that, she was gone. While I couldn't even remember why we went outside in the first place, T-Bone was humming a song from a princess movie.

"What just happened?" I asked.

"I don't know but I'm gonna sit here tomorrow at the exact same time so maybe I can see her again," he quietly whispered.

"Why would you want to see her again? She was completely rude and never once called you by your name, Sloppy Joe."

"I know," he agreed with a goofy smile. "Isn't she great?"

Oh no, I thought, T-Bone's really falling in love. Hopefully, this wouldn't become a distraction for the same kid who wanted to become an Official Ambassador, an inductee to the Hall of Fame, and a politician.

Before we could go in the house, T-Bone spotted a group of kids heading in our direction. I knew there was no way to stop him, so I sat back down.

"Hey, guys," he said as they approached, "do you mind if I ask you a couple of questions?"

"Who are you?" asked the tallest kid. I recognized him from the bus and knew his name was John, but didn't know much more about him or the kids he was with.

"I'm T-Bone," he said, "and I'm thinking about running for student council. I just want to ask you a few questions."

"I guess," the kids said at the same time.

"Okay," T-Bone began, "raise your hand if you know who the President of the United States is."

They didn't raise their hands, they just said his name. T-Bone then asked a number of questions that they didn't know the answer to and almost didn't understand the question. For Vice President they said things like Steve Jobs and Bill Clinton. The only person they could name from state government was the Governor. Most of their answers involved people they had seen on television and one boy thought Matt Lauer was the Lieutenant Governor. It was so interesting; I asked if they knew the three branches of government. One boy said maple, oak, and pine. I felt like Jay Leno when he asks people on the street simple questions. When I watched the Tonight Show, it was funny. When I realized T-Bone was right and most kids knew little about our government, I was shocked.

Before they left, T-Bone decided to ask some history questions. They knew the first president, but not one other founding father. They didn't know that the Declaration of Independence declared our independence from Great Britain and the Constitution was the law of the land. One actually said he wanted to plead the fifth but didn't even know what that meant. As we thanked them, they asked us how they did. I didn't know what to say, so I told them Benjamin Franklin's son, William, would be proud. They definitely didn't know he sided with the King during the American Revolutionary War and said, "Cool."

"Okay," I said as I shook my head. "You win. I think we'd get the same results if we asked all of the kids in our neighborhood. Maybe we should include past history, too."

"We have to explain all of these things to our fans," he said with a sense of urgency in his voice. "They have to know about our government if they're going to participate."

"I have to be honest," I sighed, "I don't think most kids are too interested in government. Maybe the problem is the word; I think it sounds too much like schoolwork."

"No, no, no," he insisted, "we have to make kids realize that the people we elect make our rules. We have a duty to know what's going on and to make sure they are doing the right thing."

"I know," I agreed, "but how do you get kids excited about politics and government when most adults aren't even interested?"

"I've got it," T-Bone exclaimed and ran back in my house.

I followed him in and he was sitting at the computer and typing in nj.gov. He grabbed a notebook and told me his plan. First, we would give Allyssa the name of elected and appointed officials in state government; like all of the senators, members of the assembly, Supreme Court justices, and the Governor. He wanted to make sure every kid knew who represented them and their family. He made a note to have Allyssa include their pictures so kids could put a face with the name.

Second, he would explain what each branch's duties were and how they worked together. Third, he would explain the two major parties so kids knew what they stood for. Fourth, he would explain the process of making laws so kids would understand it. Finally, he wanted to include something he called *T-Bone's Bill Tracker*. I knew he would get his name in there somehow.

"T-Bone's Bill Tracker will be one of the most important parts," he exclaimed. "We can track bills that affect kids, their families, schools, recreation, healthcare, and money."

"Doesn't that cover almost every bill?" I laughed.

"Not every bill, because there are thousands of them, but if we pick some of them, they can see who wrote them and how people are voting on them and where they are in the process. And they can see it in real time. We can call it *Government In Action*."

I thought about it for a moment and realized T-Bone was some sort of a genius. He wasn't trying to get adults interested; he was going for kids, the future of our state. I didn't know if it would work, but he was making me a believer. I could understand both sides of the equation. Before I moved to New Jersey, I would have failed T-Bone's test, too. The key was to figure out what made us so excited about history and government and see if that would work for other kids, too.

"I have an idea," I said. "Let's make government like a game or a sport."

"I like it!" he exclaimed. "In fact, I love it. I was thinking of something like Star Wars, but I didn't quite know how to make that go with New Jersey government. But a game or a sport, that's brilliant."

While T-Bone was hard at work and getting information for Allyssa, I decided to focus on our next adventure. Then I got my own idea. Since we were going to make government a sport, I started thinking about sports in New Jersey, particularly minor league sports. I made a list of all of New Jersey's minor league teams and was surprised that there were so many. My grandfather was a huge fan of these teams as he said they gave families a bang for their buck. I agreed. *Hopefully, T-ball would, too.*

Chapter Nine

NJ Minor League s

The more I thought about it, the more I liked my idea about sports. Actually, I liked anything that had to do with sports. Before I became consumed with New Jersey, I was consumed with sports, especially baseball. Now, I would be able to combine the three things I loved: baseball, New Jersey, and politics. It was like a dream come true, and a girl named Allyssa Barnes would make it happen.

I sat down and looked at my list of teams. It was pretty impressive. I knew about the Trenton Thunder and Camden Riversharks baseball teams and the Trenton Titans Hockey team, but I never realized just how many teams we had. My grandfather said each team was more than players and coaches; it was also an opportunity for people to spend time together. I decided that if T-Bone could suggest train stations across the state, I could suggest teams across the state.

By the time T-Bone came over the next day, I was prepared to unveil my idea. Usually, he was at my house before I knew it, before I could come down-stairs, even before I was awake. But this time was different. For the first time, I was waiting for him on the porch. It felt pretty good to be ready, to beat him at his own game. And then I heard his voice. Strangely, it came from behind mc.

"Hey, Nick, what's up?" he asked as he opened the front door and stepped outside.

"Where did you come from?" I wondered.

"Well, my mom, originally, although I'm not sure which hospital..."

"No, not where did you actually come from," I interrupted, "I meant, where did you just come from?"

"The kitchen," he smirked.

"Of course," I shook my head and got up.

Clearly, I'd have to get up pretty early in the morning to beat T-Bone to my own house. Even then, it wasn't a guarantee.

"I came up with a ton of good information about New Jersey's government," he said. "Did you know there's a website called Legiscan? You can see real bills and even see how everyone is voting."

"How did you find that?" I asked.

"It was easy. I was searching for suits, which led to suits of armor, then armored trucks, then toys, and then New Jersey legislation," he explained as if it all made perfect sense. "So then I called and talked to the boss, a guy named Sean."

"You actually called the boss at a place that follows bills in New Jersey?" I shook my head.

"No," he hummed, "I called the boss at a place that follows bills in every state and federal bills. He was really excited about what we were doing. He said something about a democracy needing informed constitutions."

"You mean constituents?" I corrected.

"That's what I said."

"No," I laughed, "you said a democracy needs informed constitutions."

"Everybody knows saying constituents is a fancy way of saying voters," he replied. "A constitution is a set of laws."

"Exactly," I agreed, "so why didn't you say that?"

"Anyway," he continued, purposely avoiding my question, "Sean said to tell him when Allyssa is finished with our website. He can't wait to see it."

"Cool," I nodded. "While you were looking up suits of armor, I came up with something interesting, too."

"You found toothpaste that will whiten my teeth faster?" he asked.

"No," I smirked. "And I am not going to stop brushing my teeth to make yours look whiter."

"Your mother bought you a new suit and you're going to loan it to me?"

"Not exactly," I shook my head, "but you're warmer."

"Really?" he asked.

"No, not at all," I laughed. "I was thinking that if we use sports for your Bill Tracker, we should use a baseball scoreboard to keep track of the votes and each step can be like the innings. What do you think?"

"I love it," he nodded. "I think that'll make it more interesting. I saw a guy named Chuck Todd who said politics is like a sport, but it's the only sport that affects your life. This is perfect."

"Great," I said. "Now, I have another sports related idea."

"If it's as good as this idea, then yes," he nodded.

"I didn't even tell you what it was," I said.

"Sorry, go ahead."

"Okay, you know how much we love sports?" I began.

"Well, for the record, you love sports more than I do," he objected. "I love sports after history, government, New Jersey, politics, and debating. But sports are definitely right after debating."

"Anyway," I continued, "you know how you thought learning about train stations all over the state would be great?"

"Yeah," he replied. "Trains are awesome."

"Okay, well, I think another good report would be about the Minor League sports teams in New Jersey," I suggested as I handed him a stack of papers. "Look at this."

I printed information for all six of New Jersey's Minor League Baseball teams. There were the Camden Riversharks, the Lakewood Blue Claws, the New Jersey Jackals from Upper Montclair, the Newark Bears, the Somerset Patriots, and the Trenton Thunder. I drew arrows to some of the important information, even how families could take New Jersey Transit to the games. T-Bone was totally impressed.

"Think about it," I said, "not only are minor league games professional players, but there are so many bonuses. You're closer to the action because the stadiums are smaller and you're near the players."

"And the mascots come around and dance with everyone," he added. "That's the best part."

"The mascot is the best part?" I asked. "You're crazy. The game is the best part, followed by the food."

"The food is good," he agreed, "and definitely cheaper than major league food. But seriously, you're not with me on the mascot thing? Do you know how hard it must be to dance in those costumes? What, do you hate mascots? Are you afraid of them?"

"Yeah, I'm afraid of a mascot," I answered somewhat sarcastically. "No, I like them just fine. I just really like the games. And don't forget the prices. The ticket prices are much less and so are the prices for parking, snacks, and souvenirs. And you know what else?"

"If you bring a camera, you can get a picture with a mascot?" he wondered aloud.

"No, the commute," I said. "My dad always says it's so much easier to get to these games."

It was decided; we would do some research on minor league teams in New Jersey. While research was always good, I also wanted to see some games. As long as they had mascots, I had a hunch T-Bone would want to go, too. Since it was still baseball season, we decided to ask my parents if we could see a game. It was easier than we thought. My dad said my mom was taking my sisters to a birthday party the next day and if the Thunder had a game, he would take us.

I looked up their schedule and crossed my fingers. If my dad could take us, along with my brother, Timmy, it would be awesome. Nine innings was a lot for my sisters. It wasn't that they couldn't sit still that long, they actually loved going to games. It was just that they couldn't stay quiet too long. Every two seconds they asked another question and if you tried to ignore them, they would squeeze your cheeks and turn your head. A game without the cackling hens, as my mom called them, would be awesome.

Not only was there a game against the Altoona Curve, but there was a box on the calendar with a small star. It meant there was a promotion. When I clicked the star it said that it was Military Appreciation Day. The team would be wearing camouflage jerseys and a group called United We Swing would provide the entertainment. It wasn't our first game, but I was so excited. I knew there would be a lot of military families and they always made me feel very proud.

The next morning, my mom and my sisters left for their birthday party while my dad made us ham and cheese omelets. T-Bone, of course, asked for French toast. Five minutes later, he was telling my dad how delicious his omelet was.

The ride to Trenton's Waterfront Park was very familiar. Since we became Unofficial Junior Ambassadors we had driven to Trenton many, many times dropping our reports off at the State House. Usually, when we entered the city, we would start asking if we could stop by the Old Barracks or the Trent House, even the State Museum. This time, however, we were focused on the game.

As soon as we pulled up, Boomer, the Trenton Thunder mascot was standing outside. T-Bone, trying to hide his excitement, was too embarrassed to run over to him. So he walked fast, really fast. After he high-fived and hugged Boomer, he stood there with his goofy electric smile.

"What are you doing?" I asked.

He didn't answer, but I could see something dangling from his wrist. It was his camera case and he was shaking his hand to get me attention. Boomer had no idea what was happening and probably wondered why T-Bone wasn't letting go.

I fumbled with the camera case and searched for the power button. When I finally got it focused, I could see T-Bone smiling from ear to ear. He looked so ridiculous. If my dad saw the picture, I knew he'd want to make it his Christmas card.

After six pictures, he finally let go and we were able to go in the ballpark. Waterfront park was right on the Delaware River and the view was pretty amazing. One of the first things T-Bone noticed was the Robert Wood Johnson Hamilton Kids Zone. Now that we knew so much about the Johnson family, we kept noticing their presence all over the state.

We spent the game cheering for the Thunder and our veterans. They went out of their way to make the military members and their families feel special and to let them know how much we appreciate their service protecting our country. In addition to feeling extremely proud and patriotic, we were also extremely hungry. Since the food was so inexpensive, it seemed like we ate all day. Since we were in Trenton, we all had pork roll and cheese, as well as popcorn and ice cream. T-Bone, of course, became friends with everyone nears us, as well as an usher named Glen.

"Is this the best job in the world?" T-Bone asked.

Glen smiled and said, "If you can't be on the field playing, this is definitely the next best thing. Are you guys big baseball fans?"

"He is," T-Bone pointed to me. "I like baseball, but he loves it."

"Me, too," he agreed. "Have you guys been over to the Sun Bank Arena for a Titans game yet?"

"Not yet," I said, "but I can't wait."

"That's great," he nodded. "You'll love it. The Trenton Titans are another great team and they're the only ECHL hockey team in the state. Maybe I'll see you there."

"No way," said T-Bone. "You work there, too?"

"I do," he laughed. "And I still get excited when the lights go down, the spotlights come up, and the music starts playing. I always get chills when the teams come out to warm up."

"I am definitely going to a Trenton Titans game," said T-Bone. "Out of curiosity, do they have a mascot?"

"Of course," he said. "Clash used to be the mascot,

but now his little brother, Rivet, has the ice all to himself. He does a great job getting people excited."

"Do you work at any other ballparks?" I asked.

"No," he laughed. "Trenton sports keep me busy and I also have a full-time job. But you should check out the other teams, also. New Jersey has amazing minor league teams like the Riversharks, the Patriots, the Bears, the Blue Claws and the Jackals."

"We already wrote it down in our notebook," T-Bone explained. "You see, we are the Junior Ambassadors for New Jersey."

"I had no idea," Glen smiled. "I'm honored to meet such important young men."

"We're not that important. We just find great places for families, visit them, and write about them for the state's website," I explained.

"Correction," said T-Bone, "now we write about them for our new website, www.nickyfifth.com. You should check it out one day. We've found a lot of great place to visit all over the state."

"I will," he promised. "And you should also check out the Rascals at the arena."

"No way," T-Bone exclaimed. "Spanky and Alfalfa are at the arena?"

T-Bone was a huge Little Rascals fan and almost fainted when he thought he could see them at the arena. I figured it must have been another hockey team. I was half right. Glen explained that the New Jersey Rascals were a professional lacrosse team that was playing their inaugural season in Trenton. Some of my friends played lacrosse and I couldn't wait to check it out. I loved that there were so many things to do in the capital of our state. Right in the middle of New Jersey, it wasn't too far for anyone to check out the history and museums before taking in a game.

We thanked Glen for all of his information and hoped we would run into him at the Sun Center. I wanted to check out all of New Jersey's teams and I was sure T-Bone would want to, also. It wouldn't be hard to convince my dad since we could probably see several games for the price of one major league game. And we wouldn't even need a coupon.

Chapter Ten

The Amazing Thomas Alva Edison

The more we explored New Jersey, the more connections we made. One person that kept popping up was Thomas Edison. I knew he was a famous inventor, I knew there was a town called Edison, and I knew he had a laboratory in New Jersey. I didn't know he was also involved in mining, was friends with Fred Kilmer, and that a boy in Rockaway was named after him. I was sure there would be many more surprises and I went right to the source for that information: thomasedison.com. On the front page was a quote from Mr. Edison that seemed to sum up his thoughts about our country.

Be courageous! Whatever setbacks America has

encountered, it has always emerged as a stronger and more prosperous nation... *Be brave as your fathers before you. Have faith and go forward.*

I also visited a great website from Rutgers called Edison.rutgers.edu and started doing my homework. It was fascinating. I learned that even though he didn't talk until he was four years old, he became the most important inventor in American history. He had 1,093 patents for things like electric power, telecommunications, sound recording, motion pictures, batteries, mining and cement. I tried to picture the world without those things and couldn't do it.

He was born in 1847 and had six older brothers and sisters. He was born in Ohio, lived in Michigan and, surprisingly, only went to school briefly. Instead his education was mostly at home by his mother and in his father's library. By 1868, he was an independent inventor in Boston before he moved to New York. He earned money working for major telegraph companies and he used that money to open several manufacturing shops in Newark, New Jersey. There it was; the beginning of his amazing work, right here in New Jersey. He was considered a first-rate inventor with inventions like stock tickers, fire alarms, and improvements in telegraph messages. Without telephones, those messages were very important and were much, much faster than the mail. As he encountered challenges with the messages, he began studying electromagnetism and chemistry. In 1876, Mr. Edison created a industrial research facility that included labs and a machine shop in Menlo Park, New Jersey on the rail line between New York City and Philadelphia.

"Hey, what are you reading?" T-Bone asked as he walked into our family room. I was so engrossed in what I was reading, I never even heard the doorbell ring or noticed that my mom let him in. Of course, since I wasn't really paying attention and since it was T-Bone, there was no guarantee that he was let in.

"I'm doing some research about Thomas Edison," I answered.

"Cool," said T-Bone. "He's a pretty important guy, you know, inventing the light bulb."

"Light bulb?" I laughed. "He invented a lot more than a light bulb."

"Did he invent lamps, too?" he asked. "Because when you think about it, a light bulb is pretty much useless without a lamp, now isn't it?"

"Look at this website," I said, getting up so T-Bone could sit in the chair.

Two minutes went by before he looked up. "Are you kidding me?" he exclaimed. "He, he, he invented the phonograph, improved telephones, and created a system of incandescent lighting. Did you know the phonograph is like the great, great grandfather of the music downloads?"

"I know," I laughed. "Think about life without his inventions. I mean really think about it. We only know about a few of them and it would be hard."

"And dark and quiet," T-Bone smiled. "It says he was known as the Wizard of Menlo Park. And don't forget he was in the first class of the New Jersey Hall of Fame."

We kept reading and learned that he left Menlo Park in 1881, creating factories and offices in NY, spending five years manufacturing, improving, and installing his electrical systems all over the world. We were both disappointed that he left, but we kept reading. That was a good thing, because we then read that, in 1887, he built his famous industrial research laboratory in West Orange, New Jersey. We also read about the Menlo Park Museum and the Art Deco Memorial Tower. I thought it was pretty cool that he was honored twice.

"Phew," T-Bone sighed. "I was getting nervous that he didn't come back. This guy couldn't lose."

"Not so fast," I said, pointing at the computer screen. "It says here that mining was his most notable commercial failure. But even his biggest failure contributed to the industry."

"And look at this," T-Bone pointed, "he changed the mining machinery to process cement. See, he made lemons out of lemonade."

We continued to read, print, and be generally amazed. My grandfather happily volunteered to bring us to his lab in West Orange and even mentioned we might be able to visit his house. We even visited the National Parks Service website and read the section called 'things to know before you come' and took notes. A couple of days later, we were on the New Jersey Turnpike, on the Garden State Parkway, and on our way to see history. We parked across the street and walked quickly toward the entrance. His labs were a National Historic Park and that was an honor they deserved.

We had plenty of questions for the ranger and he happily answered them. He told us to start with the twenty minute orientation film called the Invention Factory and then watch the 1903 silent movie called The Great Train Robbery. Next, he suggested we wander around the courtyard and learn about the Black Maria and then explore all three floors of the main laboratory building, also known as Building 5. They had audio tours, a chemistry lab, and a gift shop. The gift shop is where people purchased tickets for the lab and for Glenmont, Mr. Edison's 29 room mansion.

As much as I appreciated the information, I couldn't wait to get started. We learned that the Black Maria was the first building used for filming motion pictures. It got its name because it was large and black and resembled the old police wagons, called Black Marias. I tried to picture Mr. Edison and his workers, busy inventing the things we now take for granted.

My mom was always so impatient when she made a phone call and was put on hold; I wondered how she would have handled life before the telegraph. It probably wouldn't have been too pretty. The laboratory was huge and filled with the items Mr. Edison and his workers used to change our lives. This was one of the first research and development labs and at one time, was filled with 10,000 employees from all over the world. His researchers worked in teams and his concept was to take an invention from idea to distribution in one location. We were given audio tour headsets which meant we could stop and spend more time on certain areas we found interesting. Another ranger told us there were over 400,000 artifacts, 5 million documents, 48,000 sound recordings, 10,000 rare books, 3,000 lab notebooks, and 60,000 pictures.

The first floor was the machine shop and stock room which included tons of tools. His library was amazing and where he often entertained visitors. He was such a hard worker that his second-wife, Mina, installed a cot in the library for when he worked late into the night. On the second floor, was the precision machine shop, the drafting room, recording studio, photo lab, gallery of phono graphs, and Room 12, his private lab. As we observed everything in the lab, from all of the equipment to the actual objects, I couldn't imagine anyone, ever, being smarter than this man. Across the campus were several buildings for chemistry, metallurgy, and the pattern shop, as well as the Black Maria.

We stopped by the gift shop and I bought a book about Thomas Edison and his experiments. I thought it would be great to invent something like he did, but it didn't seem like he left much to invent.

"You know, I'd invent things, too," I told my grandfather and T-Bone, "except I think Thomas Edison already invented everything."

"At the time, he could have said the same thing," said my grandfather. "Just think about everything that has been invented since he stopped working and you'll see why he was so important."

"Light bulbs and movies," said T-Bone.

"Sure the light bulb and movies are very important," my grandfather agreed, "but his really true success was in showing people that we have to continue learning and experimenting or progress will stop. Thomas Edison was brilliant and talented, but he was also a very hard worker. His success didn't come from intelligence as much as it came from determination and perseverance."

"I guess you're right," I replied. "I wonder what Mr. Edison would say if he could see some of the things we have now; cell phones, dvd players, wireless internet, and cars."

"Oh, Mr. Edison lived to see the automobile," my grandfather laughed. "In fact, he tried to create an electric vehicle."

"Hey, they're still working on that," I said.

"And I think if he were alive today, it's not what he would say, it's what he would ask," my grandfather predicted. "I've read books about him and he was always very inquisitive, wanting to know how and why things worked the way they did."

We were so excited by the laboratory; we never even stopped for lunch. Instead we headed straight to the Glenmont Estate where he and Mina lived. It was in Llewellyn Park and a short drive from his labs. It was very impressive. Mina raised their three children in the home and we learned that he also had three children with his first wife, Mary Stilwell. They had three children, Marion, Thomas, and William and he nicknamed Marion and Thomas, "Dot" and "Dash" after the Morse Code symbols. Thomas met Mary Miller when she worked in his shop and they were married, in 1871, when she was just sixteen years old. They were married until she died in 1884. Two years later, he married Mina and had three more children, for a total of six. Their children were named Charles, Madeline, and Theodore. Of all of his children, Charles was the most public and even served as Governor of New Jersey from 1941-1944.

"Look at this place," T-Bone remarked.

I wasn't sure exactly what he was referring to, because it was all awesome. The house was amazing and the stories were great. They showed us his office, overlooking the yard, where he played Parcheesi. It was funny when our guide told us if he started to lose, he changed the rules. When we left the house, we checked out the garage. This is where we saw the 1922 Model-T car that Henry Ford had given him.

"He sure had some famous friends," I noticed.

"He was a very important man," my grandfather explained. "He wasn't important because he was rich, he was rich because he did important things. There's a lesson to be learned there."

"What's the lesson?" T-Bone innocently asked. "Invent things and become rich, right?"

"No, that's not even close," my grandfather shook his head. "The lesson is that people should be considered important because of their character and accomplishments, not because their parents are rich or famous. Every time I turn on the television I see people called celebrities and they haven't actually done anything important or that requires talent. We need to start celebrating intelligence and achievement, we need to support people who make a difference, whether they're creating new technologies or curing diseases. We should raise the standards we have for being impressed and expect more."

My grandfather had a point. We never see the scientists that create the medicines we take or the inventors and creators of the things we use every day. We never hear enough about the soldiers that perform heroic acts to protect our country. If we did celebrate all of these people, they'd certainly make great role models.

"If I become a businessman, I want to do it like the Mr. Edison or General Robert Wood Johnson," I said. "I want to make employees important and I want to create things. Maybe I'll even have a credo like General Johnson."

"You know who else had a credo?" my grandfather asked.

I gave it some thought, gave up, and then shook my head. He happily told me Thomas Alva

Edison's credo:

Be courageous, try everything until something works and dedicate yourself to your passion, trusting that what you are will show in what you do.

I'm definitely getting a credo, I thought.

Chapter Eleven

Pine Hill & Clementon Park

After our Thomas Alva Edison adventure, I was excited that we now had our own website. When our reports went on the state website, it was just the reports and some pictures. Now, as long as we had Allyssa, we could really bring New Jersey to life for kids. T-Bone came over to talk about his campaign and I felt bad that I kept ignoring it. It wasn't that I didn't care; I was just really wrapped up in New Jersey. When he said he was coming over, I promised we would only work on the campaign. And I really meant it.

School would be starting soon and I knew we had to get a jump on this. T-Bone had all of the information about running for student council in a binder and I assumed he had read it all. He hadn't. He came in with a bag full of stuff, his suit, and an electric smile.

"Hey, how'd you get out of your house in a suit?" I

asked. "I thought your mom said to stop wearing your good suit."

"I snuck out in it," he said.

"How can you sneak out in a suit?" I wondered.

"Anything to win," he said with a big grin. "I put a sweatshirt and sweat pants over top of it. Then when I got to your house, I hid in the bushes and took off the top layer. Pretty clever, huh?"

"Why didn't you just take that stuff off when you got inside?" I asked.

"Good point," he said. "Anyway, look what I got."

One by one he pulled items out of a bag. Each one was more ridiculous than the other. First, he pulled out a Vote For T-Bone bumper sticker with a picture of him on the side. He was wearing the suit, his teeth were sparkling and his hair was slicked to the side.

"What is this?" I asked.

"It's a campaign bumper sticker," he said, as if I had just asked him the most stupid question ever. "You see voters put them on their cars and other drivers read it and then they vote for me."

"Problem," I said, "your voters are way too young to drive and you really don't need other drivers to know about you. Plus, that girl, Wanda, might have been right; this bumper sticker might make people think they're voting for their favorite steak or their favorite steakhouse."

"Okay," he paused as he rifled through the bag, "how about this?"

"What is it?" I asked. "It's sample of T-Bone's Sweet chocolate bars."

"You printer stickers to put over candy bar labels?" I asked.

"Well, these are all just samples," he explained. "I would never make a decision like this without my campaign manager."

"Why," I shook my head, "would you want to say you're sweet? Don't you want people to think you're smart and that you have good ideas?"

"This is for the girl vote," he said. "I think girls want to vote for someone they think is sweet and nice."

"Holy moly," I gasped, "you can't actually say girls only vote based on sweetness and not intelligence. And you can't possibly believe that, do you?"

"Well, what do you want me to give them?" he demanded. "I have Have a Ball with T-Bone mini soccer balls for boys who promise to vote for me."

"What?" I said. "Are you trying to buy votes? This isn't how you run a campaign. I thought we were going to talk about your platform, you know, your ideas to make our school a better place."

"I have to get elected before I can make changes," he defended his ideas. "I can wait until after I'm elected to tell them what I'm going to do. Right now, I have to razzle dazzle them."

"Wait until after you're elected?" I asked. "Who waits until they're elected?"

"A lot of politicians," he insisted. "I have been watching the news and some of them say they'll wait until they're elected to let people know their plans. I guess it makes it more mysterious."

"No, no, no," I pleaded with him, "this isn't an episode of Scooby Doo. There's no mystery. We have to run a real campaign and you have to get the voters, you know the kids our age who don't drive, to be interested in what you have to say."

I grabbed his bag and was horrified when I started pulling things out. He even printed T-Bone coupons that promised he would do certain things if people voted for him. One offered to mow the grass and rake the leaves, and another offered to do a homework assignment. For someone who loved politics as much as T-Bone, I couldn't believe how bad his campaign ideas were.

I grabbed a notebook and started asking him a bunch of questions, writing each answer down.

"Why do you want to be on student council?" I asked. "And the real reason, not the reasons you think people want to hear."

"Because I want to be a leader," he said softly and somewhat embarrassed. "I want to look for ways to make school better and then find ways to make that happen."

"Perfect," I said as I wrote it down. "Next, what ideas do you have?"

"Well, middle school can be intimidating," he began, "so I thought we should partner older kids with new kids and this way everyone will have someone they know around school. I'd also make parents have to come take an anti-bullying class with their kids if their kids are bullying people. And I want to make sure each kid knows New Jersey Transit is one of the best ways to get around, but to be safe when they're near the tracks. We have to help Grace and Barb."

"Great," I said. "All good ideas. What else?"

"I think we should have more clubs so kids can try more things. We need clubs that let kids use their hands," he explained. "You know some kids get really good grades, but some kids don't. It doesn't mean they're dumb; they just may have other talents that no one knows about."

"I never thought about that," I admitted. "Next."

"I have a lot of ideas," he said. "But don't you remember last year? There wasn't even a debate. It was just a bunch of kids giving things away to get people to vote for them. It was more about popularity."

"Okay, so change that," I suggested. "That is most definitely not a way to run any campaign, even in a school, and definitely not the way for schools to teach kids about government."

"I don't know, Nick. I don't think I can," he said. "I won't get one vote."

"Don't be silly," I said. "I'll vote for you."

Before we could get any further, my dad came in and made an unusual request. He had the day off and wanted to know if there were any places we needed to visit. I told him about the letter from Aniah Wilson who wrote about Pine Hill, New Jersey, Clementon Park, and the Tomlinson House. He said it was a good idea. I asked T-Bone if he had a bathing suit on under the suit. My dad looked at me like that was a really dumb question. I didn't feel like explaining that, since T-Bone wore an entire sweatsuit over a real suit that a bathing suit could have been under there, too.

"Listen, T-Bone," I said, "go home, get a bathing suit and we can still plan your campaign while we're driving there. Plus, we can ask my dad for some advice."

T-Bone ran home and exactly nine minutes later, was back in the family room. He almost got ready faster than I did and he had to run home. Before we got in the car, I grabbed the information Aniah sent us. She said the town was named because of the many pine trees and I thought that made perfect sense. It also had the highest elevation in Camden County, at 214 feet, so I figured that's where the Hill part came from. According to Aniah, the views from Pine Hill allowed people to see the entire area, as well as the Philadelphia Skyline.

We decided to stop by the Mayor's office to learn more about the town. Since most small towns didn't have a Visitors Center, we found that Mayor's offices were always happy to help. This was no exception. We met Mayor Green and he told us about the town and how it was originally part of Old Gloucester County, incorporated in 1695. In 1903, they became part of Clementon Township. Over the years they were even called Mount Ararat and Clementon Heights. In 1929, they finally became the Borough of Pine Hill. People used to come to Pine Hill for vacation and health reasons, as it was considered to have a healthy climate. He suggested we ride by the Pine Hill Fire Department and also check out Veteran's Memorial Park which honored the men who served in WWII.

A very interesting fact was that they had the only ski mountain in south Jersey. In the winter, it was called Ski Mountain and, for a while, in the summer, it was Action Mountain Water Park. While 214 feet didn't sound like much, we saw a picture from the 1970s and the mountain was packed.

"Can people still ski there?" I asked. "Do you still have the water park?"

"No," said the Mayor, "not anymore. "That land was turned into the Pine Hill Golf Club, which also had impressive views from the course."

"Wow, Ski Mountain is now the Pine Hill Golf Club," I said.

"Not exactly," he answered. "It's now a Tom Fazio designed course called Trump National Golf Club. I'll give you directions so you can ride by it."

"Can you tell us about the Tomlinson House?" asked T-Bone. "Anaiah wrote about it."

"I'm sure she did," he said. "The kids in our town are very protective of that house, but sadly it's not in good shape. Built in 1834, the Tomlinson House is the oldest structure in Pine Hill and was home to one of the county's most prominent families."

But when he told us about the condition of the

house and efforts to save it, I knew T-Bone wouldn't be happy. The only thing worse than the historic homes and mansions that were already demolished was the knowledge that one was on the 10 Most Endangered List just because of money. We decided to write about it and hoped that the attention would help save and restore the house. We figured it couldn't hurt.

"You see, if I was a podiatrist," T-Bone whispered, "I could pay for all of the repairs myself."

"I think you mean philanthropist," I corrected, "a podiatrist is a foot doctor. And you can't save every endangered landmark."

"When I'm a Senator I'll make that part of my platform," he said. "And then when I save all of these places, I'll be inducted into the Hall of Fame. If I do enough good deeds, maybe the home where I spent my childhood home will become a museum one day."

"Oh, you mean my house?" I joked.

The Mayor overheard us and said, "You know, what you boys are doing could be even more valuable than money. By getting people excited about history and seeing these places, you're affecting the attendance numbers. And when those numbers remain steady, most landmarks have enough funds to support themselves."

We thanked Mayor Green and headed toward the Memorial Park, the Fire Department, and Trump National on our way to Clementon Park. Trump National Golf Course was a private course, so we really just saw the sign. Unfortunately, that was more than enough to make T-Bone furious.

"Hey, hey," he hollered. "Stop the car! That sign is wrong. That is a ridiculous sign and it's wrong!"

My dad and I knew exactly what he was referring to. The sign read Trump National Golf Course, Private, and then, the word that sent T-Bone over the edge, *Philadelphia*.

"Why does that sign say Philadelphia?" he asked as if he were the first person to see it. "How could they put up a sign with a mistake? Didn't they proofread it? This golf course is in New Jersey!"

"I don't think it was a mistake," said my dad. "I think they put that there on purpose because it's part of the Philadelphia Metropolitan area."

"Yeah, the part that's in New Jersey," said T-Bone.

"If it's good enough to be in New Jersey, shouldn't New Jersey be in the name? This is an outrage!"

"He has a point," I said. "I mean, I'll always love Philadelphia, but it should say *New Jersey*."

"Add that to my platform," T-Bone said, as if I walked around with a clipboard, chronicling his every thought. "I will propose a law that awesome places, because I'm sure it's an awesome place, that are in New Jersey, must say New Jersey."

"Duly noted," I said, as if I had written something down. Hopefully, the amusement park would make him forget that he was furious with Mr. Trump.

Our next stop was Clementon Park, one of America's oldest amusement parks. At over 100 years old, the new owners spent millions of dollars to update the park, including an enormous wave pool for the water park. I wasn't sure where to go first so we decided to ride the rides and then hit Splash World. Clementon Park wasn't the biggest park in the world, but it was just right. It was the kind of place that a family could relax and have a great time. My dad was so comfortable that he decided to take a break and let T-Bone and I meet him at a certain time. That was one of the first times that had ever happened.

The park was set against Clementon Lake and while the lake was only used for non-motorized activities, it was mostly a really cool background. We went on the Ring of Fire, the Thunder Drop, King Neptune's Revenge, the Sea Dragon and the Flying Pharoah. By that time, we were warm and decided to check out the 23,000 square foot Big Wave Bay wave pool. I loved the combination of swimming pool and Jersey Shore. After that, we hit the Torpedo Rush, and the Vertical Limit Racer.

"Are you guys ready to go?" asked my dad.

"No way," said T-Bone. "We didn't hit the faves yet."

"What are you talking about?" I asked.

"You know, the faves, the favorites, the most traditional amusement park rides," he explained. "The carousel, the train, the ferris wheel, and the pedal boats."

"He's not serious, is he?" asked my dad.

I didn't have to answer. I knew the answer, my dad knew the answer, and T-Bone was now in line for the train. But, I had to admit it, they were fun also.

We ended up staying much longer than we thought we would and definitely longer than we promised my mom. I wasn't too worried, though, because when she heard about our day, she couldn't possibly be mad that we were late for dinner. Especially when T-Bone didn't even notice.

When we returned home there was an envelope sitting on the kitchen table. Inside was a photo book called the Island of the Wildwoods by the 2011-2012 Margaret Mace Fourth Grade. It was filled with colorful pictures and descriptions of their favorite Wildwood places. They even included an interesting fact for each location.

Wow, I thought, it's like the Wildwoods have their own ambassadors. Then I looked at the last page explaining how the idea for the book was inspired by me and T-Bone. I was speechless. The students, the school, and the Home and School Association worked together to produce the photo book with an organization called Lunch With Lynch. I was really curious, so I did a little research.

Lunch with Lynch started out with a man named John Lynch reading to students and turned into an organization that supports all of the Wildwoods' students. He even ate lunch at the Glenwood Avenue School once a month and often invited

Mayor Troiano, Judge DeWeese, police officers and firefighters. I couldn't wait to share the website www.lunchwithlynch.com with all of our fans. I wondered how long until there was a *Lunch with T-Bone*!

Chapter Twelve

VOTE FOR T-BONE

After our visit to Pine Hill and Clementon Park, I knew it was time to get serious about T-Bone's election. Summer was over and we were back in school. Everyone kept saying they couldn't believe how fast summer had flown by. I, on the other hand, couldn't believe how many adventures we actually had.

We started working with Allyssa on the website and she was great. She loved our ideas and turned them into something real. Well, she loved most of our ideas; at least my ideas. T-Bone came up with some doozies. There was the lunch and dinner countdown clocks and the petition to make mini golf a medal sport in the Olympics. But he did have one great idea. During the first week of school, he met with Mrs. Swanson, the moderator of our school's student council. He asked her if they could talk about changing the way student council was run. He presented his ideas in his usual T-Bone, smooth-talking style and the meeting went very well.

T-Bone suggested that every student who wanted to run for council submit their ideas for the whole school to review. He asked that the school prohibit kids from giving gifts away to get other kids to vote for them. And he wanted to school to host a debate where all of the candidates could share their ideas. There was no guarantee that this would turn the election into a real election as opposed to a popularity contest, but Mrs. Swanson loved the idea. It was her first year serving as moderator and one of her own goals was to change the format. She couldn't believe a student had such solid ideas and supported every single suggestion. She even added one that T-Bone hadn't thought of; she wanted to hold an election assembly to explain how student government should work. I thought it was brilliant.

By the second week of school, we were all called to the gym for a surprise assembly. Mrs. Swanson had created a power point that explained how a democracy works. She explained that the biggest threat to a democracy was voters who are uninformed and do not participate. She showed pictures of our founding fathers and explained the Constitution and the Bill of Rights. Then she showed our website that introduced kids to the New Jersey's Senate, Assembly, Governor, and Supreme Court with pictures of our elected officials. I was shocked to see everyone looking at our website. Then she gave a conclusion that moved everyone.

"Boys and girls," she began, speaking softly. "You live in an amazing country with an amazing form of government. This is a government of the people, by the people, for the people. As you get older and become more politically aware, you will hear adults say that the system is broke and cannot be fixed. You will hear people say there's no sense in voting because votes don't count. You will hear people say that you must be rich to be involved in politics. In a democracy, this does not need to be a permanent condition. You have enormous rights in this country, but you also have enormous responsibilities. You must make the effort to know what the issues are and form your opinions based on truth and fact. You must use your voice, a voice that citizens in many countries do not have, and you must participate. Whether it's a federal election, a state election, or even a student council election, you must be involved and know the issues. We are changing the way we run our student council elections. Students who wish to run for office will share their ideas with you and we will hold a debate so the student body can understand the candidates' positions. We will no longer allow candidates to distribute gifts to encourage students to vote for them. This will be an election based upon ideas. During the next two weeks, you will hear from each candidate and you will be invited to submit questions to be asked during the debate. If you believe you can make your school a better place, I encourage you to run for student council. If you do not wish to run, you will still have an obligation to be informed and participate. The right to use your voice is the biggest gift the founding fathers left you. Use it wisely."

The room was quiet. Mrs. Swanson left everyone speechless. I looked around and everyone was moved. Suddenly, student council had taken on a new meaning and T-Bone started it all. Later that day, Mrs. Swanson invited students who wished to run for office to visit her room and sign up. T-Bone was the first in line. I stood outside her classroom, hoping to catch a glimpse of the competition. One by one, students lined up outside her door. I saw

Brian Langston, Kendall Roberts, Jessica Reynolds, Dalton Harris, and Wanda. I didn't know her last name, but I sure remembered her. She was the politically aware girl T-Bone quizzed in front of my house. She was also the girl that made him speechless. This could be a problem, I thought.

"Hey, did you see everyone who wants to run for office?" he asked with a big goofy smile.

"Yeah, I saw her," I said. "But you cannot let her distract you. I'm serious, you have to stay focused."

"No problem," he nodded. "Did you smell her hair? It smelled like strawberries. I love strawberries."

Oh no, I thought. He noticed her hair smelled like strawberries. This wasn't good. As his campaign manager I didn't know what to do to keep his head in the game. I doubted any other campaign manager ever had to deal with their candidate falling in love with an opponent. My only idea was to make sure he was super prepared.

That night, after we finished our homework, we started preparing ideas for his platform. It was refreshing that the election would be about ideas instead of who gave out the best t-shirts. But now, we had to deliver. We made a list of the things he realistically thought he could accomplish.

1. Mentor program for all new students.
2. Bullies would attend the anti-bullying program with their parents.
3. More clubs that allowed kids to explore areas that aren't actual subjects.
4. Senior citizen tutoring program.
5. Healthier lunches and interesting fruit.
6. Community service projects.
7. A school wide garden in the courtyard.
8. Train safety.

I loved every idea he presented and it felt like a real campaign. He filled out the form Mrs. Swanson gave each candidate and explained each idea. Even though she was impartial and not allowed to favor any student, she did tell T-Bone he had solid ideas and was elevating the campaign. He smiled for the rest of the day. Another amazing development also happened. He started looking normal. He stopped using his mom's bronzing lotion and whitening his teeth. He hung up his good suit and stopped slicking his hair to the side. I felt like he was in a good position. Then, Mrs. Swanson called each candidate to the main office to share each of their ideas during morning announcements.

Jessica Reynolds went first and promised to limit the number of binders we lugged around each day. It was a sizable number of binders and I knew kids would like that one. She also said she would install televisions in the cafeteria so kids could relax during lunch. I figured that wouldn't go over too well with our principal or the school board. She also suggested that students be allowed to text in class. That one worried me. She knew the school would never allow it, but that was her way of trying to get kids to vote for her. Hopefully, most kids would see through it.

Kendall Roberts had some good ideas. First, she promised a suggestion box for student input and e-books instead of text books. I loved the idea of carrying one tablet around instead of heavy text books, but that sounded expensive and probably wouldn't happen. Then she said she'd like to see more projects about current events. It was a good idea, but as soon as she said more projects, I could hear the whole school start groaning.

Dalton Harris loved science and every idea was about improving the science lab. They weren't bad ideas, but I doubted there would be that many kids who only wanted better science equipment. It was a shame, though, because Dalton was probably going to grow up and cure something and this could have made that happen quicker.

T-Bone went next and spoke very clear, so I assumed he couldn't see Wanda. I could only judge the reaction of the classroom I was sitting in, but everyone really liked his ideas; especially since he didn't propose more projects.

Brian Langston was introduced next and we all waited for him to start speaking. After about ten seconds, everyone started looking at each other, wondering if our speaker suddenly broke. But after a minute of silence we heard Mrs. Swanson thank him. Unfortunately, Brian was really, really quiet. Apparently he was so quiet; a microphone couldn't even pick up his voice. At least we could read his ideas later.

Finally, Wanda Heiss, was introduced. She was clear, calm, and focused. She also had good ideas. She requested two more minutes in between classes so students could deposit books in their lockers rather than carry loads of heavy books and binders all day. She suggested cameras on buses and a zero tolerance policy for kids who caused problems. She wanted to create a Student Volunteer Corps and a class cause. She explained the volunteers would complete tasks at home and in their neighborhoods and the money they earned would go toward a cause selected by the class. She wanted to meet with a different homeroom every morning to get feedback and invite everyone into the process. She also wanted to invite local senior citizens to be a part of the school community.

Holy Moly, I thought. For a moment, I wasn't even sure who I would vote for. For the rest of the week, politics was the main conversation at school. T-Bone and Wanda appeared to be in a dead heat for first place. We knew it would be a tight race and started preparing for the debate. We wrote down his ideas and then talking points for each one on index cards like my grandfather suggested. We had stopped by our friend, George's house to weed his landscaping and he gave us the same talking point idea, so it must have been good. He also said he was really proud and was expecting big things from both of us.

The night before the debate, T-Bone was a little nervous and I assured him that nervous was normal. In fact, I would have been concerned if he wasn't a little nervous. I wasn't too concerned, though, because I knew that speaking in front of a large crowd would energize T-Bone. I just hoped he wasn't within smelling distance of Wanda's hair. I even entertained the idea of secretly spraying her hair with broccoli water or something equally awful. But we promised a clean campaign and he would have to win on his own merit, even if his opponents hair smelled like a banana split.

The next morning, we filed into the gym and took our seats. This was the first time any of us were attending a Student Council debate and everyone was excited. Mrs. Swanson was the moderator and she began by reviewing the rules of a debate for the candidates and the audience. Each candidate was allowed one minute to introduce him or herself. T-Bone had an impressive resume since he was the only one who had a business and was about to become an Official Junior Ambassador for New Jersey. After the introductions, Mrs. Swanson started asking the questions. Poor Brian, no one could hear any of his answers. Jessica must have had stage fright and said the word um about 45 times. Dalton did well when discussing science, but was kind of lost when the questions were about anything else. I think he lost the audience when he tried to explain the water cycle. Kendall was a great speaker but for every question, her solution was giving each student a tablet. Clearly, her parents refused to buy her one.

Then there was T-Bone and Wanda. They both gave great answers and they were both calm and cool. I didn't know how people scored debates, but according to my calculations, this was a dead heat.

"Wanda, why do you think the student body should vote for you?" asked Mrs. Swanson.

"I believe in government," she began. "On any level, government is the foundation for our lives. We need leaders who respect democracy and put the people they represent ahead of their own interests. I promise to do that. I promise to make hard decisions that mean something, not just decisions that make me more popular. For example, we have a real problem with the school budget each year as many of the senior citizens in town vote the budget down. If we invite senior citizens to come into the school and provide extra assistance to students, they'll feel like a part of our community and want to see us succeed. Plus they've got so much life experience that would benefit all of us. Kids spending more time with senior citizens is good for everyone."

"And Tommy, why do you think the student body should vote for you?"

"I agree with my opponent 100%. I am very close with several senior citizens and I think it's a great idea. Clearly, we both believe strongly in welcoming senior citizens to our school."

Oh no, I thought. He must have smelled her hair. What was he doing? He didn't even answer the question, he just gave her a compliment. I wanted to yell, "Stop the debate!"

"That's very generous of you, Tommy," said Mrs. Swanson. "But why would they vote for you?"

"Well, a leader has to have character," he said. "That's what you do when you think no one is looking. A leader has to have ideas, but at the same time, listen to what the people want. For example, American kids have an obesity problem, but it's not just about weight. It's about being healthy. We serve fruit in the cafeteria, but an apple or orange isn't as exciting as a bag of chips. But, maybe a fruit-kabob with berries and grapes and pineapple is. And maybe really colorful salads could be more exciting than fries. And maybe if we have a school garden, not only will we will learn a valuable skill, we'll be more excited to eat the things we have grown. These are creative solutions to real problems."

Phew, I whispered to myself. Nice save.

Wanda continued to hit each question out of the park, but so did T-Bone. Wanda explained the need for the extra minute or two in between classes and it really made sense. And who could argue with her idea for a Student Volunteer Corps? It was a brilliant idea that not only made the school look better; it would also make each student who participated better.

T-Bone clearly explained his position on each of his ideas. He discussed his ideas about senior citizens without sounding like he was repeating what Wanda had said. He then discussed bullying programs that parents must attend and mentoring programs as if he was a seasoned speaker. The reason he sounded so smooth was that he truly believed in what he was saying. He even managed to discuss train safety so it wasn't scary and just made sense. Then he spoke about adding more clubs.

"It would be nice if every student could easily achieve straight A's," he began, "but that's not realistic. Some kids will be more successful in areas like math or science, some may be great writers, but some kids may not be. Those same kids may be really great with their hands and would benefit from learning things like wood shop, auto repair, agriculture, landscaping, cooking, computer repair, or anything else that they are drawn to. There are so many laws that limit what can be taught and we have to challenge those laws.

Middle school is where students should start exploring different options for their future. Let's create clubs and then classes that provide really valuable skills for everyone."

And with that, we heard the beginning of a loud, solid clapping from the back of the gym. Then we could see that same gentleman stand up and continue clapping. I leaned toward the aisle and instantly recognized him. It was Billy from the State House and everyone followed his lead. T-Bone got a standing ovation. He stood at the podium, smiling from ear to ear. I turned to see Billy give T-Bone a thumbs up and a big smile before he slipped out the side door.

When the debate was finished, each student was able to vote. Mrs. Swanson was very smart and played another power point video with patriotic music and great pictures as one row at a time voted. She did this to keep kids from discussing how everyone should vote. She wanted every single student to cast their vote based upon the information they learned from the debate.

I looked up at T-Bone while he sat on the stage and gave him a thumbs up. He gave me a cheesy, politician's wink. We'll definitely have to discuss that later, I thought.

At 2:00, Mrs. Swanson paged all of the candidates to the main office. Brian was in my math class and he quickly left the room.

"Good afternoon, everyone," she said over the loud speaker. "I want to take a moment to commend every student today. I am very proud of all of our candidates. Each one ran a campaign of character and integrity and handled the stress of a debate beautifully. So, now, based upon the votes, I will name the candidates and the positions they have won. At-Large Council members who will represent the entire school are Brian Langston and Jessica Reynolds. Student Council Treasurer is Dalton Harris and Secretary is Kendall Roberts."

My heart was racing. I knew the positions were based upon votes. The highest votes won the following positions in this exact order: President, Vice President, Secretary, Treasurer, and At-Large council members. There were only two spots left, President and Vice President.

"Boys and girls, we have a very unusual outcome for the position of President and Vice President that I will now share with you. There was only a two vote difference between Tommy Rizzo and Wanda Heiss. I have met with both students and the student with the highest number of votes has made an unheard of first official decision. That student has decided not to have a Vice President, but rather, a Co-President. So the Presidents of the Student Council will be Tommy Rizzo and Wanda Heiss. In addition, they have decided not to disclose who had the higher number of votes. Thank you for your participation in the political process and please, do not forget to use your voice. But please do so, respectfully."

I didn't know what to say. How could this happen? Co-Presidents? Who had ever heard of Co-Presidents? Which one had the most votes? My mind raced to figure this out. If Wanda had the most votes, I doubt she would have shared her presidency with a kid she compared to steak. T-Bone on the other hand, was all about rules and regulations and if he won fair and square, I couldn't imagine him giving it up either. When we got off of the bus and walked to my house, we were finally alone and I was able to ask him.

"What happened?" I asked.

"Can't say," he smiled.

"Yeah, yeah, yeah, you can't say," I nodded. "I'm your campaign manager. I have a legal right to know."

I didn't know if he would buy the whole legal right to know thing, but figured it couldn't hurt. He looked like he was considering it.

"Okay," he took a deep breath, "but only because it's the law, we decided since the race was so close and we both really liked each other's ideas, we should work together."

"I get it," I agreed. "But who gave up president?"

"No one gave it up, one more person got it."

"Okay, who had the most votes?" I demanded. "Just tell me who had the most votes. Who was the winner? Just give me the first or last name of the winner."

"Listen, at the end of the day, everyone's a winner. The students get two people with good ideas to lead and we're both really happy. Does it really matter who got the most votes?"

"Actually, yes, it does." I insisted. "It completely and totally matters. At this moment I cannot think of anything that matters more. T-Bone, I'm not kidding. I am your campaign manager and I need to know."

"I'm sorry, Nick," he said, "I promised to never tell anyone, ever. But I will say this...*her hair smelled awesome today.*"

Welcome to the
Franklin Mason Press
Guest Young Author Contest

Turn this page for stories from our three Guest Young Authors, ages 9-12 years old. From the thousands of submissions, these stories were selected by a committee for their creativity, originality, and quality.

Franklin Mason Press believes that children should have a paramount role in literature, including publishing and sharing their stories with the world. We hope you enjoy reading them as much as we did. If you would like to submit a story you have written, keep reading after the stories. Enjoy!

And the winners are...

1st Place Guest Young Author

Jakiere Legoskey
John Glenn ES
Pine Hill, NJ

Adventures of Nicky and T-Bone

The adventures of Nicky and T-Bone show why Pine Hill is a perfect place to visit. The boys were visiting nearby Clementon Park, founded in 1907 by Theodore Gibbs. The park had attractions that included a theater, dancing casino, roller coaster, steam carousel, and a Razzle Dazzle ride.

Clementon Park is on Clementon Avenue and the boys heard the cheerful screams all around. Nicky and T-Bone went on the Torpedo Rush ride. Next was the water ride that stands at a sky-scraping 60 feet tall. They climbed into the launch capsule to count down to the most thrilling water slide. They rode the safari train that had a unique mystery and the magic of an African desert.

Nicky could smell hot, steamy food and his stomach started to growl. "Should we get something to eat?" Nicky asked T-Bone.

"Sure," said T-Bone as they walked up to the counter and ordered their food. Nicky ordered a hot dog, T-Bone ordered a burger and they both ordered lemonade. They were stuffed after eating their food and as soon as they finished their drinks, they left Clementon Park with a buttery popcorn and a cotton candy. They were talking about how much fun they and decided to visit the oldest structure in Pine Hill, just up the road from the park. The Tomlinson House was built in 1790 by the Tomlinson brothers and an addition was added in 1844.

The house stands on Blackwood-Clementon Road. The cooking supplies they used in the 1800's were bizarre! By the way, in my opinion, if you look at 1800s clothing it looked terribly comfortable. It looks like all the women were getting squeezed to death and the men wore big hats like Abraham Lincoln wore. Nicky whispered to T-Bone, "What do they store in their hats? Nuts?" T-Bone quietly laughed and moved around the historic house.

They learned a lot about Clementon Park and Pine Hill's Tomlinson House and the adventurous boys realized Pine Hill was a great place to visit.

2nd Place Guest Young Author

Anna Salvatore
Toll Gate ES
Pennington, NJ

The Last Day of School

I'm sitting at my desk, waiting.

My eyes are fixed on the slowly moving hands of the clock. The teacher has been talking but today I will not listen.

Today is the last day of school. My desk will soon be empty, the halls will soon be filled with happy kids running, but I'm not listening to the never-ending drone of the teacher.

Instead, I must sit on my old, small, blue chair, hearing the   Principal's high heels coming down the hallway. Click, clack, click, clack. Now, I know that she is doing her routine rounds.

Everyone around me is fidgeting in excitement. I can barely sit still. The clock is like our King and we are like servant's in its Kingdom. When the summer bell rings, we are set free from our spell and released into summer. It has been a year since I have tasted Summer, and I hope it is worth a school year. The bell is ringing, and it is now my favorite sound.

Here comes vacation!

3rd Place Guest Young Author

Kaitlyn Blaylock
John Glenn ES
Pine Hill, NJ

Nicky's Pine Hill Adventure

It was just like any other boring old night for Nicky because he just got back from another day trip. As soon as they got home, Nicky and T-Bone went inside to Nicky's messy bedroom and went to sleep. The next morning, after they ate breakfast, Nicky's mom told them they would be going to Pine Hill. "You have to be kidding me. Who would ever want to go to Pine Hill? I bet it's not even that great," said Nicky.

Nicky's mom had said that they would be at the Tomlinson House all day long. After that, Nicky's mom told them that it was built in 1834 and it's a museum. They left at 8:00 in the morning and they were on their way. When they arrived they asked some of the local residents about the Tomlinson House. The residents said they loved it, so it was clear that they would go.

When they went to look at the Tomlinson House they saw a sign that said Now Open To The Public on it. They walked up the creaky old stairs, went inside, and saw many things. They went upstairs to see all of the old bedrooms and walked around the house. When it was 2:00 pm, they left for the day. They didn't get home until 8:00 pm because they stopped at Friendly's for dinner. Perhaps Nicky enjoyed the day trip this time!

Nicky Fifth's New Jersey Contest

Are You A New Jersey Character?

Submit your favorite New Jersey destination to Nicky Fifth and T-Bone and you could become a character in an upcoming Nicky Fifth book. Write a 3-4 paragraph persuasive essay, selling your idea to Nicky and T-Bone. Make sure your idea is located in New Jersey and hasn't been included in a previous book in the series. Check the website for a list of places already included.

Entries are judged on creativity, writing style, history, and level of persuasion. Do not list numerous locations; focus on one and make sure it is located in New Jersey. To enter, visit www.nickyfifth.com and be sure you have your parents' permission.

Prizes:

1st Prize - $200.00 Barnes & Noble Gift Card
  YOUR idea is used in an upcoming book
  YOU become a character in the book

2nd Prize - $100.00 Barnes & Noble Gift Card
  YOUR idea is used in an upcoming book

3rd Prize - $75.00 Barnes & Noble Gift Card
  YOUR idea is used in an upcoming book

Nicky Fifth's New Jersey Contest Winners

1st Place- Alexi Garcia
(*pictured on the back cover*)
A.C. Redshaw School, New Brunswick, NJ
The City of New Brunswick, NJ

2nd Place (tie) - Olivia Cella
Alpine School, Sparta, NJ
Sterling Hill Mine, Ogdensburg, NJ

2nd Place (tie) -Delaney Sniffen
Alpine School, Sparta, NJ
Sterling Hill Mine, Ogdensburg, NJ

3rd Place - Aniah Wilson
John Glenn School, Pine Hill, NJ
Pine Hill Township and Clementon Park

Nicky Fifth's
Race to the State House

As Nicky Fifth and T-Bone patiently await the Senate and General Assembly votes that will name them Official Junior Ambassadors, students all over the state participated in the Race to the State House contest. Classes and small groups submitted their most creative ideas to let state legislators know that New Jersey needs Nicky and T-Bone.

The entries were amazing and creative and Nicky and T-Bone appreciate everyone's support. Throughout this story you will meet the fourth graders from Katherine D. Malone School in Rockaway. They are the first place winners and their prize included a pizza party, Barnes & Noble gift cards, and each student becoming a character in this story.

You will also meet our second place winners from harrison Elementary School and our third place winners from Delaware Township School.

Nicky Fifth's Race to the State House
Contest Winners

1st Place
Katharine D. Malone School
Rockaway, NJ
4th graders
Mrs. Jaremack, Mrs. Beck,
Mrs. Frauenpreis, Mrs. O'Donnel

2nd Place
Harrison Elementary School
Livingston, NJ
Mrs. Orozco's students
Jimmy Souffront
Michael Petrillo
Jake Cohen
Josh Minion

3rd Place
Delaware Township School
Sergeantsville, NJ
4th graders
Hailey Becker
Marissa Matteo
Lauren Bruhl

From Lisa Funari Willever's

Writers Workshops

Write about topics that you know about or things you enjoy. If your story is going to be interesting, you need to be interested in your topic.

Use details when describing your characters and your setting. You want your readers to feel like they've known your characters their whole life. Characters are more than just boys or girls with your friend's names. You should build your characters with creative likes, dislikes, and unique qualities. When it comes to your setting, use your words to paint pictures. Use your senses to bring your setting to life. Your readers should feel like they have been to your setting.

Read your story out loud and really LISTEN to it! If you listen closely, you'll find many things that you would like to change or improve.

Keep an idea notebook and whenever you get a great idea that you don't have time to write about, jot it down. Index cards in an index card box (or even a shoe box) are great places to keep ideas safe and handy.

When looking for spelling mistakes, don't trust your eyes or computers, read each line backwards, like the editors do!

Many children's magazines and websites publish children's work, so always be on the look out for places to submit your stories.

When you submit a story, always, always, always follow the directions. Each magazine, publisher, or website will have their own rules and it is important that you follow them.

If your school or local library has a writing club or offers workshops, join in. These are great places to share your work and get new ideas. If your school or library doesn't have one, start one!

After you submit your story, don't wait by the mailbox, start your next story and after that, start your next story, and after that...well, you get the picture.

And, of course, enjoy writing!

About the Nicky Fifth Foundation

In May 2015, after years of providing tens of thousands of free books to schools and children in need, Lisa Funari-Willever created the Nicky Fifth Foundation to promote literature, education, and awareness for New Jersey children.

With the help of her husband, Todd Willever, and good friend, Iris Hutchinson, the Nicky Fifth Foundation was born. The first step was establishing a dynamic Board of Directors to guide the foundation. Luckily, Lisa knew many dynamic people.

One by one, all of the board seats were enthusiastically occupied by individuals who really care about New Jersey kids. Along with Lisa, Todd, and Iris, the Board of Directors consists of Paula Agabiti, Karen Funari, Dawn Hiltner, Don Jay Smith, Walker Worthy, Brenda Zanoni, and Nancy Byrne.

Once the board was established, the first program, Nicky Fifth's CODE READ, began.

NFF

Nicky Fifth Foundation

CODE READ

by the Nicky Fifth Foundation

In the Nicky Fifth series, you will read about Nicky Fifth's CODE READ and you may assume it's pure fiction; a good idea, but pure fiction. Well, it was a great idea, and it really happened. The Nicky Fifth Foundation worked closely with the Trenton Fire Department and their unions, FMBA Locals 6 and 206, the New Jersey Education Association, FEMA Corps, the Mercer County Prosecutors Office, churches, and numerous individuals and volunteers to collect over seven thousand children's books.

Working out of Trenton Fire Headquarters, books were sorted and bagged. A bag was prepared for every Pre-K through 5th grade teacher in all fifteen Trenton Public Schools. This massive operation was completed in five weeks. Starting on June 23, 2015, CODE READ spent two days delivering books to every public school in the city.

As a caravan of on/off-duty firefighters and volunteers, led by fire vehicles, wound through the city, children saw their heroes responding to a very different type of crisis. With four out of five city libraries closed for over five years, CODE READ saved the day.

But providing books to keep was just the very first step: Phase 1. Three weeks later, the firefighters worked with the Nicky Fifth Foundation to implement Phase 2 and place books in three Trenton firehouses. City children can now check out the firehouses while they check out a book. Through the Nicky Fifth Trenton Firefighters' Book Club, children receive a library card, borrow books, and get to know the heroes in their neighborhood.

Phase 3 places firefighters in the schools, on a regular basis, to read with students. This not only shows students how important reading is, it creates a greater sense of community.

As the first CODE READ city, Trenton has welcomed the program and thoroughly supports the foundation's work. But, this is just the beginning. The Nicky Fifth Foundation plans to expand to other cities in need across the Garden State. We invite students, teachers, and families to join our effort and ensure every New Jersey child has books at home and easy access to borrowing books.

If you or your school would like to join Nicky Fifth's CODE READ or our other vital programs, visit www.nickyfifth.org. Get informed, get involved, and change lives!

Nicky Fifth Curriculum

The Nicky Fifth Curriculum brings New Jersey and vital topics currently omitted from test-based curriculums to life. Through humorous, realistic fiction, the Nicky Fifth series allows teachers to present numerous topics to students within the context of literature, eliminating the need for additional instruction time. As opposed to current trends, the Nicky Fifth curriculum encourages teachers to embrace their creativity and adapt lessons to address the needs of their students.

Teachers can seamlessly combine literature with topics such as New Jersey history, geography, civics, government, the environment, the art of debate, education, poverty, and wellness in an age-appropriate manner. Using the familiar Nicky Fifth characters, this unique Jersey-centric curriculum spans grades 2-6, is easy to implement, is inexpensive, and easily lends itself to extension activities. Schools purchase the chapter books and Nicky Fifth provides amazing multi-discipline materials for all learners, at no cost.

Visit **nickyfifth.com** to easily access over 400 printable worksheets, dozens of slide shows, and exciting videos...*all at no cost!* Enjoy!

About the Author,
Lisa Funari Willever

Lisa Funari Willever wanted to be an author since she was in the third grade and often says if there was a Guest Young Author contest when she was a child, she would have submitted a story a day. *Maybe two a day on weekends!*

She has been a wedding-dress-seller, a file clerk, a sock counter *(really)*, a hostess, waitress, teacher, and author. While she loved teaching in Trenton, New Jersey, becoming an author has been one of the most exciting adventures of her life. She is a full-time mom and a *night-time author* who travels all over the world visiting schools. She has been to hundreds of schools in dozens of states, including California, South Dakota, Iowa, South Carolina, North Carolina, Florida, Delaware, Connecticut, New York, Pennsylvania, West Virginia, Ohio, Nevada, Idaho, Utah, Alabama, Louisiana, and even the US Navy base in Sasebo, Japan.

Lisa has written over two dozen books for children and even a book for new teachers. Her critically acclaimed *Chumpkin* was selected as a favorite by First Lady Laura Bush and displayed at the White House, *Everybody Moos At Cows* was featured on the Rosie O'Donnell Show, and *Garden State Adventure* and *32 Dandelion Court* have been on the prestigious New Jersey Battle of the Books List. Some of her titles include *You Can't Walk A Fish, The Easter Chicken, Maximilian The Great, Where Do Snowmen Go?, The Culprit Was A Fly, Miracle on Theodore's Street, A Glove of Their Own, There's A Kid Under My Bed,* and *On Your Mark, Get Set, Teach.* Her Nicky Fifth series has been embraced by New Jersey schools and a unique and innovative Nicky Fifth curriculum has been developed.

Lisa is married to Todd Willever, a Captain in the Trenton Fire Department, and they have three children, Jessica, Patrick, and Timmy.

Lisa was a lifelong resident of Trenton and while she is proud to now reside in beautiful Mansfield Township, she treasures her 34 years in the city. She is a graduate of Trenton State College and loves nothing more than traveling with her family, reading, writing, and finding creative ways to avoid cooking!

T-Bone's Bill Tracker

BTt

Visit nickyfifth.com to check
out T-Bone's Bill Tracker.
Click on
Government In Action
to track your elected officials.